The Moors of Andalusia: The History of the Muslims in the Iberian Peninsula during the Middle Ages

By Charles River Editors

Alhambra from San Nicolas Square

Introduction

Ajay Saresh's picture of a courtyard in the Alcázar

The term Moor is a historical rather than an ethnic name. It is an invention of European Christians for the Islamic inhabitants of Maghreb (North Africa), Andalusia (Spain), Sicily and Malta, and was sometimes use to designate all Muslims. It is derived from *Mauri*, the Latin name for the Berbers who lived in the Roman province of Mauretania, which ranged across modern Algeria and Morocco. *Saracen* was another European term used to designate Muslims, though it usually referred to the Arabic peoples of the Middle East and derives from an ancient name for the Arabs, *Sarakenoi*. The Muslims of those regions no more refer to themselves by that term than those of North Africa call themselves Moors. Maghreb, or *al-Maghreb,* is a historical term used by Arabic Muslims for the territory of coastal North Africa from Alexandria to the Atlantic Coast. It means "The West" and is used in opposition to *Mashrek*, "The East," used to refer to the lands of Islam in the Middle East and north-eastern Africa. The Berbers refer to the region in their own language as *Tamazgha*. In a limited, precise sense it can also refer to the Kingdom of Morocco, the proper name of which is al-Mamlakah al-Maghribiyyah, "Kingdom of the West."

The history of the Spanish Peninsula is closely bound to that of the Moors. The term "Spain" was not in wide use until the region was united by the monarchs of Aragon and Castile, and the Moors called the lands they ruled in the Iberian Peninsula Al-Andalus, traditionally thought to be an Arabic transliteration of Vandal, the Germanic tribe which briefly ruled the region in the early fifth century. The English name Andalusia derives from the Spanish Andalucia, which is still used by Spain to name its southern region.

Not surprisingly, three religions attempting to coexist during medieval times resulted in nearly incessant conflicts, marked by high taxation, disparate societies, rigid cultural controls, and systemic violence. Despite the odds, these three religions managed to live in a state of quasi-acceptance and peace in most of the major cities in the Iberian Peninsula like Cordoba and Toledo, with sporadic warfare occurring on the borders between Al-Andalus and the Christian kingdoms near the Pyrenees Mountains. Muslims, Christians, and Jews would attempt to reorganize their societies several times over the centuries through warfare, always with Jews on the lower rungs and Christians and Muslims fighting it out above them.

Though it's often forgotten today, the fighting that took place during the *Reconquista* was not originally driven by religion. Instead, the majority of the battles were fought by ambitious rulers who sought territorial expansion, like many other civilizations during the Middle Ages. In fact, the *Reconquista* would not gain its unique religious flavor until the 13th century, when the territories that would become Castile and Aragon drummed up religious fervor to achieve its aims and gained papal support from Rome.

While the Moors have always been associated with Spain due to their lengthy stay on the Iberian Peninsula, the most famous battle they were involved in was actually fought in modern France. While the Franks were consolidating a kingdom there, Muslim forces were pushing out of North Africa and into the Iberian Peninsula in the early 8th century, and by the dawn of the 730s, the Umayyad dynasty had expanded its territory from the Atlantic to the Pyrenees, a series of seasonally snow-capped mountains in Europe that forms a border between the nations of Spain and France. This would lead to Charles Martel's most famous military victory came at the Battle of Tours, also called the Battle of Poitiers, on October 10, 732. At this battle, a united Frankish force decisively defeated the invading Umayyad Caliphate, making it one of the most important in all the Middle Ages for stemming the advancement of the Islamic forces in Europe.[1] As historian William E. Watson put it, "Had Charles Martel suffered at Tours-Poitiers the fate of King Roderick at the Rio Barbate, it is doubtful that a "do-nothing" sovereign of the Merovingian realm could have later succeeded where his talented major domus had failed. Indeed, as Charles was the progenitor of the Carolingian line of Frankish rulers and grandfather of Charlemagne, one can even say with a degree of certainty that the subsequent history of the West would have proceeded along vastly different currents had 'Abd ar-Rahman been victorious at Tours-Poitiers in 732."

---

[1] Frankfurter, 122.

The Moors of Andalusia: The History of the Muslims in the Iberian Peninsula during the Middle Ages

The Spread of Islam

The death of Prophet Muhammad, the founder of modern Islam, in Medina on June 8, 632 shook his followers to the core. His disciples, dispersed across southern Arabia, Persia, Ethiopia, and parts of the Byzantine Empire, collectively mourned the loss of their guiding star, and like many other religions, cracks immediately emerged in the bedrock of the Islamic faith following his death. Shortly thereafter, the religion suffered its first great schism, otherwise known as the "Sunni-Shia Divide."

The rival denominations concurred on a few principles. They agreed that Allah sent Muhammad, his final messenger, to the mortal realm to reinvigorate and further propagate the age-old, yet neglected theology which they believed was the true, prototypical religion practiced by Adam, Ibrahim (Abraham), Musa (Moses), and other early prophets. Both the Shiites and Sunnis partook in prayer five times a day, fasted during Ramadan, performed charitable acts, and dutifully embarked on pilgrimages to Mecca, as dictated by the Five Pillars of Islam. Only by dedicating their lives to praising Allah and adhering to His word would they be granted entry through the gates of Paradise.

After that, however, the two branches failed to agree on much of anything else, and given the absence of a supreme authority to clarify canonical laws and settle disputes, the prophet's followers developed and pursued their own interpretations of the Quran. Initially, the torch was passed on to Abu Bakr As-Siddiq, an intimate companion and the father-in-law of Muhammad through the prophet's third wife, Aisha. But many of the subjects inherited by Abu Bakr, the first Rashidun caliph, vehemently protested against the coronation, and the candidate of their choice was 32-year-old Ali ibn Abu Talib, who was Muhammad's blood cousin (the son of his paternal uncle) and the husband of the prophet's daughter, Fatimah. Those in Abu's camp became the Sunnis, who now comprise 85-90% of the 1.6 billion Muslims across the world today, predominantly located in Saudi Arabia, Egypt, Jordan, and Indonesia. The Shiites, whose loyalties lay with Ali, make up the remaining 10-15%, around 154-200 million, and are mostly based in Iran, Iraq, Syria, Turkey, Azerbaijan, Yemen, Palestine, and Lebanon.

The word "Shiite" was a derivative of the aptly-named "shia," or "The Party of Ali." Ali's adherents argued that the right to reign over the whole Muslim community solely belonged to the direct descendants of Muhammad, and Ali was the prophet's closest male relative and thus the true Imam. They believed they were the ones who were qualified to decipher, defend, and uphold Islamic law and Muhammad's hadiths. The term "Sunni," on the other hand, stemmed from the phrase "Ahl ah-Sunnah," meaning "People of the Tradition." Sunnis favored a more democratic approach; occupants of the caliphate's throne were to be determined by vote, cast by an electoral council (Shura) consisting of top-ranking religious officials across the Islamic Empire. Ancestry alone, they contended, should not determine who was caliph; instead, experience, profound piety, mastery of the Quran, and robust leadership skills were the necessary merits.

From Abu Bakr, the Rashidun Caliphate was turned over to Omar I, Muhammad's father-in-law via his fourth wife Hafsah, whose reign was abruptly cut short in 644 when he was slain by a Persian slave. The prophet's son-in-law Uthman ibn Affan, husband of his daughters Ruqayyah and Umm Kulthum, served as the third caliph until his untimely death in 656, this time prompted by Egyptian rebels. Ali's time came at last, much to the delight of the Shiites, but alas, he, too, would suffer the same fate.

It was the insurgents who unceremoniously handed Ali the caliphate on a platter, and needless to say, his detractors took issue with this transition, with some audibly accusing him of orchestrating Uthman's murder due to the lack of action taken to punish the fallen caliph's killers. Ali's short-lived reign was punctuated by civil wars, most of them waged by Uthman's cousin Muawiya, then the governor of Syria. To break the stalemate at the Battle of Siffin the following year, a panel of judges was jointly selected to determine the victor. The judges ruled in favor of Muawiya, who then pronounced himself the true caliph.

Ali cried foul, resolutely rejected the verdict, and resumed his rule from his new capital in Kufa, Iraq. In late January 661, three Egyptian Kharajites (a new, separate sect composed of those who detached themselves from Ali when he consented to the tie-breaking arbitration at Siffin, as "judgment [belonged] to God alone"), led by Abd-al-Rahman ibn Muljam, snuck into the Great Mosque of Kufa. The intruders crept up behind Ali, who was halfway through his Fajr prayer, unsheathed their poison-glazed swords, and swung at the oblivious caliph. Ibn Muljam's accomplices missed, but his blow nicked Ali on the crown of his head, and within 48 hours, Ali was dead.

Muhammad's grandson Hasan, the oldest male among Ali and Fatimah's children, was chosen to fill his father's shoes, taking his place as the fifth Rashidun caliph. As expected, Muawiya balked at the council's decision and challenged Hasan. Six months of heated correspondence, internal turbulence within the Rashidun camp, and grueling negotiations later, Hasan agreed to step down on the condition that Muawiya pledged to leave the appointment of the next caliph to the Shura.

Muawiya established a new dynasty, the Umayyad Caliphate, and reneged on their pact, declaring his son Yazid the heir to his throne. This did not sit well with Hasan and his brother Husayn, who would have been the most promising contenders, and their sentiments were echoed by the Shiites. They had refused to bow before the three Rashidun caliphs and would do the same with the Umayyad kings in Damascus and later the Abbasids in Baghdad, pledging their allegiance to Ali, Hasan, and Husayn – the first, second, and third Shia imams – instead.

Fully aware of the Shiites' insubordination, Muawiya sought to stamp out the growing threat as soon as possible. Hasan was poisoned to death by one of his wives, Ja'da bint al-Ash'at, at Muawiya's behest in 670. Husayn was killed by Yazid himself, who was crowned the second Umayyad caliph 10 years later, at the Battle of Karbala (Iraq) in 681. The deaths of the three

Imams gave rise to the concepts of martyrdom and Shia-style grieving. Shia Muslims continue to honor Husayn on the anniversary of his death in a yearly ritual known as the "Ashura," which sometimes features self-mutilation, self-flagellation, and other modes of religious self-harm.

The massacre of the Talib tribe at Karbala left the Shiites prostrate with grief. Of the 72 people who perished from Husayn's party, 20 of them were Talibs, among them Husayn's brothers and his six-month old infant, and all of whom were decapitated. Unsurprisingly, the Shiites' animosity towards the Sunni caliphs and officials, along with those of other Islamic persuasions, became further inflamed, and as evidenced by the Day of Ashura, was a traumatic watershed moment for the medieval Shia Muslims.

The consequences of the Karbala incident were not lost on Yazid. Sensing retribution on the horizon, the oppression and abuses suffered by the Shiites grew exponentially. Like Muawiya, who singled out and slaughtered thousands of Talib sympathizers and their families and seized land, jewels, and other valuable property from dissidents on a regular basis, Yazid finished off several of Husayn's surviving ambassadors, relatives, and companions. The Umayyad army also defiled the mosques in the hallowed cities of Medina and Mecca, butchered hundreds of thousands of Muslims, and raped countless women in these holy metropolises.

Inevitably, the steady proliferation of Shia Islam in the following centuries generated more rounds of hostile infighting on a larger scale within the community. This, in turn, spawned a number of radical factions, including Ismailism, the precursor to the Order of Assassins' Nizari Ismaili faith.

Orthodox Shiites paid tribute to 12 Imams. The last Imam, Muhammad al-Mahdi, more famously known as the "Hidden Imam," mysteriously vanished in 940. According to the so-called "Twelvers," al-Mahdi never died but was instead instructed by Allah to stash himself away in a cave under a mosque in Samarra, an event referred to as "The Occultation." The "Messianic Deliverer" was prophesied to reemerge at the end of time, whereupon he would reclaim control of the Islamic world and restore justice and peace on Earth.

The Ismailis, or "Seveners," disaffiliated themselves from the Shiites after the death of the sixth Imam, Jafar al-Sadiq in 765. Jafar's third son, Musa al-Kadhim was appointed as the seventh Imam. Not all were content with the council's choice; some Shiites, who would become the Ismailis, had been banking on al-Sadiq's eldest son, Ismail (hence their name), and adamantly repudiated al-Kadhim's authority. Since the Ismailis' worldview was centered on hard-line egalitarianism, they were strongly opposed to the heathen lifestyles, shaped by excessive extravagance and debauchery, of the Abbasid caliphs. To garner recruits for the grassroots cult and raise awareness for the new movement, obviously outlawed, the Seveners dispatched da'is, who were essentially secret missionaries, to various cities and villages near and far.

The Ismailis' political pull reached its peak in 909 when Ubaydulla, a Sevener scion of the Muhammad-Talib family founded the Fatimid Dynasty, the first Ismaili caliphate. The Fatimid Empire was headquartered in Al-Kahira (now Cairo), which translates to "The Victorious," and in its prime, consisted of territories in Persia, Syria, Sicily, other parts of Western Arabia, and Central Asia.

While the Muslims across the Arabian Peninsula engaged in internecine warfare, Islam struck at the Middle East and Africa like a thunderbolt over the coming centuries, and unlike Christianity, Judaism and Zoroastrianism, the other monotheistic religions of the region, it was spread by force of arms as a matter of course. Islam does not accept forced conversion any more than Christianity does, but the concept of *jihad*, a sacred war for the defense of Islam, became the doctrine even during the lifetime of the Prophet Muhammad. The concept of defense was interpreted in a broad, pre-emptive sense to allow Muhammad's followers to conquer the Arabian Peninsula and to invade the lands of the Persian and Byzantine Empires. Religion was probably not the primary motivation, however. Arabia possessed limited arable land, water and resources, while the fertile plains of Syria, Palestine and Mesopotamia lay temptingly to the north. The peoples they conquered were generally permitted to keep their religion and laws so long as they paid the *dhimmi*, the tax imposed on non-Muslims which was considerably higher than that paid by Muslims. That was the prescription of Koranic Law. In practice most adopted the religion of the conqueror to avoid paying the tax and for the social and commercial advantages adoption of the state religion conferred.

Jihad figures strongly in the history of Islam and indeed is a continual feature of the struggles of the great Moorish empires that spread across the world. There is a tendency in modern scholarship to emphasize jihad as a spiritual and internal struggle toward perfection, but as the historian David Cook noted, "In reading Muslim literature—both contemporary and classical— one can see that the evidence for the primacy of spiritual jihad is negligible. Today it is certain that no Muslim, writing in a non-Western language (such as Arabic, Persian, Urdu), would ever make claims that jihad is primarily nonviolent or has been superseded by the spiritual jihad. Such claims are made solely by Western scholars, primarily those who study Sufism and/or work in interfaith dialogue, and by Muslim apologists who are trying to present Islam in the most innocuous manner possible."[2]

As with so many other civilizations, warfare brought material advantages. Islam did not allow the enslavement of Muslims, but it did permit non-Muslims to be enslaved as prizes of war, so the use of slavery, already endemic to pre-Islamic Arabia, became entrenched in Islamic society. Islam also retained polygamy and concubinage from polytheistic Arabic societies, and sexual slavery was common. Slaves were expected to convert to Islam, though strictly speaking they were not supposed to be compelled. Life as a slave for an Arab master was not always oppressive - talented men might become trusted stewards of their lords' estates or even government

---

[2] Cook, David (2005). *Understanding Jihad*. University of California Press.

officials. The lot of women was more onerous, as Islamic jurists allowed masters to use their female slaves as they wished. A select few women might become legal wives and enjoy considerable status and privilege.

Despite the burdens and indignities imposed on conquered peoples, Islam also brought certain advantages, at least to the Arabs and Muslim converts. All members of the Islamic faith community, the *Ummah,* were equal before Allah, and all, whether prince or pauper, were bound to observe Allah's law. The highest lord who acted unjustly might be condemned publicly and even deposed, and the meanest of subjects could not be forbidden from appealing to the law of Allah against his sovereign. Islam taught compassion toward the poor and disadvantaged, the essential dignity of every human before Allah, and religious toleration. The Islamic government was based on the concept of *al–Shura* ("consultation"), and rulers were counselled by jurists to govern with deference and respect to the needs, advice, and opinions of their subjects. Of course, these lofty principles were not always observed, and their dereliction played a significant role in the history of the Moors.

Muhammad was considered the earthly head of the Ummah, and when he died, his father-in-law Abu Bakr was elected *Khalifah* ("Caliph, Successor"). The caliph was not a kind of pope or emperor - he had no power to interpret the law of Allah, only to enforce and protect it. The task of interpreting the law in particular circumstances belonged to the *Ulema*, a kind of college of Islamic jurists who published their judgements as *fatwas*. A fatwa superseded the decree of the caliph and could even depose a ruler perceived to be defying the Ulema.

Although the caliphate was initially led by Arabs, the force that bound their empire was not ethnicity but religion. As Edward Gibbon put it in *The History of the Decline and Fall of the Roman Empire*, "Under the last of the Umayyads, the Arabian empire extended two hundred days journey from east to west, from the confines of Tartary and India to the shores of the Atlantic Ocean ... We should vainly seek the indissoluble union and easy obedience that pervaded the government of Augustus and the Antonines; but the progress of Islam diffused over this ample space a general resemblance of manners and opinions. The language and laws of the Quran were studied with equal devotion at Samarcand and Seville: the Moor and the Indian embraced as countrymen and brothers in the pilgrimage of Mecca; and the Arabian language was adopted as the popular idiom in all the provinces to the westward of the Tigris."

The caliphate first invaded Africa in 639. Egypt was rich, fertile, and the breadbasket of the Byzantine Empire, and after the fall of Alexandria, the Arabs proceeded in 642 to conquer Cyrenaica and Tripolitania (Libya). It was there that the army stopped, despite an eagerness to proceed, for fear of losing control of Egypt, so it was not until 647 that a fresh army attacked the Roman Exarchate of Africa Byzacena (modern Tunisia) and parts of Mauretania and Numidia. The Byzantine Empire was divided in a religious conflict, and Exarch Gregory had declared independence, not only in support of Christian orthodoxy but also in light of the emperor's inability to defend North Africa. Gregory died at the Battle of Sufetula and the Byzantines withdrew to their fortresses before 20,000 Arabs. The invaders were unable to overcome the defenders' strongholds and withdrew from the exarchate in return for hefty amounts of gold.

In 661, Mu'awiyah of the Umayyad dynasty seized the caliphate from Hasan, grandson of the Prophet Muhammad. The new caliph was more interested in extending the rule of Islam into Anatolia and Asia, and it was not until 670 that an Arab army renewed the invasion of Africa. By this time, the Byzantines, severely mauled by the invasion of 647, were incapable of extending their authority beyond the coastal cities such as Hippo Regius (modern Annaba) and Carthage. The vacuum was filled by a number of autonomous Christian Romano-Berber states. The greater part of Mauretania (Algeria and Morocco) was already ruled by Berber kingdoms (Altava and Quarsenis) which gained independence after the Vandal invasion of the 6th century. Queen Dihya of Jerawa Zenata Berbers ruled a kingdom in the Aures Mountains and resisted the Arab invasion for five years. Though it is known that Dihya existed, most other details are the stuff of legends. The Muslims, no doubt surprised by her strength and ability to defeat the armies of Allah, believed her to be a sorceress, but her eventual defeat at the Battle of Tabarka around 702 ended Berber military power. By this time the Arabs had taken the Byzantine strongholds, including Carthage, which the Arab general Hassan razed to the ground. Icosium (Algiers) fell in 700, and nine years later the invaders reached the Atlantic coast.

The Arab conquerors called their new dominion *al-Maghreb*, "The West" and they established their base at Tikirwan in what is now Tunisia (called Kairouan by the Arabs). Recognizing the tenacity of the Berber tribes based in the Numidian Highlands, they formed alliances with them, dangling the prospect of Byzantine booty before them. These Berbers, consisting of Christians, pagans, and Jews, mostly accepted Islam, and thus was born the Arab-Berber union that established the people known to Europe as the Moors.

The Moors of the Caliphate

The Muslim leaders of Arabia believed the caliphate should be an Arab empire. The teachings of the Prophet proclaimed the equality of all believers, but they did not know how to translate that into reality and non-Arab converts were treated as second-class Muslims little better than unbelievers. Indeed, the Umayyad caliphs treated the Berbers as if they were infidels, imposing on them the *dhimmi* tax and exacting tributes of slaves. This was not simply ineptitude - it was a direct contradiction of Islamic law and the cause of much unrest throughout the caliphate.

This policy was a result of attempting to maintain the Arabs as the ruling class. The burden of taxation fell upon the non-Muslim subjects, but as these converted, the pool of revenue rapidly diminished and the Arabs therefore saw that they had no choice but to impose the *dhimmi* even on converts. The proud Berbers took the imposition especially badly, particularly as they had been promised a share in the caliphate's wealth in return for converting and swelling the ranks of its armies. In the invasion of the Iberian Peninsula (Chapter 4) the Arab governors of the

Maghreb gave the Berbers the most onerous tasks but a lesser share in the spoils than their Arab masters. In 718 Caliph Umar II recognized the threat posed by hostile Berbers and other non-Arabs and forbade the levying of *dhimmi* on them, but his successor Hisham, faced with military reversals, reimposed it in 724 by duplicitously claiming that it applied not to persons but to their lands.

The policies of the Umayyads were met with resistance, and religious movements began to emerge advocating their overthrow and the reform of the caliphate on the basis of the equality of all peoples and fidelity to the law of Allah. Local revolts broke out, especially in Andalusia (Muslim Spain) and in 721, Yazid, the Arab governor in Kairouan, was assassinated after reimposing the hated tax even before Caliph Hisham had done so himself.

The last straw came in 740 when Omar, the deputy governor of Tangiers, decreed that the Berbers in his district were to be considered conquered people and thus subject to confiscation of property and enslavement. The tribes of western Mauretania rose under their leader Maysara al-Matghari. At the time, the bulk of the Arabic-led army was engaged in Sicily and Tangiers was conquered and the hated Omar killed. Maysara proclaimed himself caliph and unleashed a series of campaigns down the length and breadth of the land now called Morocco, killing the Umayyad governors as he went.

The Arab Governor of Maghreb in Kairouan, Ubayd Allah, immediately recalled his forces from Sicily. Dissensions within the Berber camp led to the overthrow of Maysara, and his replacement Khalid annihilated a force of cavalry sent to contain the Berbers at Tangiers until the Sicilian force returned. The encounter became known as the Battle of the Nobles, for it effectively destroyed the Arab aristocracy.

Habib, commander of the force that was to invade Sicily, returned to Africa to find it in a state of panic. He could do nothing but entrench himself at Tlemcen (western Algeria) and send to the caliph at Damascus for reinforcements. In February 741, Caliph Hisham dispatched some 30,000 men under the command of a new governor of Africa, Kulthum ibn Iyad al-Qasi. The bulk of this army was made up not of Arabs but Syrians who maintained an ancestral disdain for the ruling Arab class, and their presence was considered almost as unwelcome as that of the Berbers. The Syrian commanders treated Arab and Berber alike with contempt, and it took all of Kulthum's diplomatic skills to prevent an uprising against them.

The Syrians were confident that they would smash the Berber rebels, whose army probably numbered 200,000. The Syrians and Arabs combined only numbered 70,000, but many of the Berbers had no armor and were only armed with knives. They shaved their heads in the manner of religious fanatics and appeared to Kulthum to be disorganized and undisciplined. But Habib and the few remaining African commanders urged against engaging the Berbers in open battle and counseled defensive tactics instead. But the governor would not hear of it, and urged by his Syrian underlings set out to engage the rebel army. The two armies met at Bagdoura, near modern Fez, in October 741.

From the very beginning of the fighting, it was evident that Kulthum and the Syrians had seriously underestimated the Berbers. Skirmishers armed with slings and bags of pebbles succeeded in unhorsing the elite Syrian cavalry, and those who came to the aid of the unhorsed warriors were likewise ambushed. The Berbers drove horses maddened by water bags and leather straps tied to their tails into the Syrian cavalry, creating confusion. What remained of the cavalry array rallied and furiously charged the Berbers on foot, only to discover that the infantry parted to allow them to pass through their lines. They then closed, separating the horsemen from the infantry. The bulk of the Berbers then fell upon the infantry while a rearguard fended off the separated cavalry. The Arab and Syrian commanders were specifically targeted, and after the bulk of them were slain, the lines collapsed. The Syrian cavalry too succumbed and a general rout ensued. Almost 40,000 perished, including Governor Kulthum and Habib, the general who had counseled against the battle.

The Umayyads did not long survive the Battle of Bagdoura and in 747 a Persian general, Abu Muslim, led a revolt against the dynasty. It was widely supported by both Arabs weary of mismanagement, corruption and military reversals, and by non-Muslims promised equality. At the Battle of Zab (January 25, 750) in Mesopotamia, Abu Muslim defeated Caliph Murawan II and was proclaimed caliph himself. Thus began the reign of the Abbasids, so-named after Mohammad's uncle Al-Abbas ibn Abd al-Muttalib, from whom Abu Muslim claimed descent. Establishing his court at Baghdad rather than Damascus, the new caliph proclaimed the end of the Arabs' privileged status, de-centralized the caliphate, and brought non-Arab Muslims into government.

The re-energized Caliphate regained a measure of control over the province of Africa (Tunisia and eastern Algeria) but in Mauretania the Berbers remained independent. Several states emerged in the lands now called Morocco. The largest and most powerful of these was established by Idris, a survivor of the Battle of Fakhkh (near Mecca, June 11, 786), whereby the Abbasids suppressed an attempt to install Al-Husayn ibn Ali, another descendant of the Prophet Mohammad, as caliph. Idris was himself a descendant of the Prophet, and he built the city of Fez and established himself there as emir. He is commonly regarded as the founder of the Moroccan state, though the name itself would not be used until much later. The Idrisids coaxed Arab settlers back to the region and used Arabs as viziers (ministers), thus renewing the union of Arab and Berber but on more equitable terms. Under the Idrisid emirs, the progenitor of the Moroccan state dominated the region until 927.

The Arrival of the Moors in Spain

Humbly sized Iberian tribes called the "Turdulos," said to be the most civilized of all the inhabitants in the region at the time, made their homes in Granada since as early as 2000-1500 BCE. They cultivated and bred communities on the land bordering what would one day become the colorful, thriving city. To the Turdulos, however, home was Ihverir. In this growing city, the Turdulos lived alongside the Phoenicians, their neighbors' small colonies scattered along the coastline.

In 550 BCE, the decades' worth of peace and harmony in Ihverir was disrupted by the unforeseen invasion of the Carthaginians, who hailed from the ancient city of Tunis in Northern Africa. The reins of power were soon prised out of the Phoenicians' grasps, and fell snugly into the palms of the Carthaginians. A blended city known as Elybirge would soon arise from the ashes.

Approximately three centuries later, the Romans descended upon Elybirge, and once again, control of the city switched hands. The Romans transformed the town into a municipality, placing it under authority of a local government. The city was re-branded in Latin as *Florentia,* meaning "city full of flowers or fruits." Understandably so, this intriguing city, covered with lush meadows, handsome forests, glistening greenery, and sensational scenery, was one that everyone had their eye on.

While Iliberis was under Roman rule, the lack of attention and security designated to the city made it easy for those watching on the sidelines to swoop in when the city was at its most vulnerable. The breaking point came in the 5th century, and during the slow but definitive crumble of the Roman Empire, it would not be long before the Visigoths sniffed out a new opportunity. The Visigoths, a term used to describe nomadic Germanic tribes, had a poor reputation among the Greeks and Romans. They were scorned as uncouth "barbarians," and were condemned for being "different" and "unsophisticated." Be that as it may, the Romans appeared to have no qualms when it came to allying with the Visigoths. It was said that the ensuing Gothic invasion of Spain, France, and Italy had been orchestrated by the Romans, a last-ditch attempt by an empire wobbling on its last legs.

The takeover of the Iberian Peninsula – the second largest peninsula in the continent, encompassing most of Portugal, Spain, Andorra, and a slim slice of France – was not a single operation but instead required efforts by the Roman-sponsored migrations of the Sueves, Alani, Vandals, Visigoths, and other tribes. The Visigoths first set foot on the peninsula in the year 416, where they were tasked with forcefully re-instituting Roman authority upon other Germanic invaders who had occupied the land. Initially, the Visigoths followed instructions to a tee, but as time progressed, it appeared that there may have been reason to have been suspicious of the Visigoths after all. In 418, they were relocated to France, where they established a makeshift kingdom of their own in Toulouse. When they inevitably wisened up to their employer's increasingly fragile authority, they realized it would not take much to squeeze the disintegrating empire out of the picture.

In 429, as the Vandals retired to Africa, the Visigoths poured back into Spain and claimed the land. Artifacts and records that have survived from the Visigoth (or as historians call it,

"Invisigoth") period that would have shed light on the accurate statistics of the population under their rule are extremely limited. Not much can be surmised from the smattering of coins, medals, gold, and silver left behind during this mysterious period.

Though their actual contributions cannot be ascertained, a few conclusions have since been drawn. As opposed to the Vandals, the Visigoths were thought to have been more effective rulers, as the town rapidly flourished in size and populace. For the first time, Granada became home to a military base. Meanwhile, the trend of Christianity had also begun to spread its wings. The Visigoths' strengthening of their military has led many to believe that Granada had served as a capital for the province, even back then. Around the same time, a small colony of Jews would also immigrate into the corner of the city and claim that nook as their own, named "Garnata al-yahut."

In the Visigothic empire, the king was elected by "aristocratic peers" as the "chief" of the people. Not only did he defend the interests of his subjects, he served as the general of war. To unify the religion in the kingdom, the law that allowed intermarriage between Visigoths and Hispano-Romans was repealed, as they hoped to consolidate the city in Arianism. Arianism was a Visigothic rendition of Christianity, one that saw Christ as a great prophet, but disregarded the belief of the Holy Trinity. This period of Arianism did not last long, and following Visigothic leaders soon declared Catholicism the official religion of the kingdom.

The Visigoths remained in power well into the early years of the 8th century, but many attempted to wrestle the area away from them. All of these attempts would eventually fizzle out, with one important exception. The Muslim or Umayyad Conquest of the Iberian Peninsula was first mentioned in a Christian source, the *Chronicle of 754*, penned that same year. While the book's contents were vague, it made references to a conquest that was characterized by "expressions of horror and grief." Somewhat paradoxically, the same account also painted the same invaders-turned-governors as "legitimate rulers."

The majority of the theories behind what had incited the seemingly impromptu conquest has revolved around four different scenarios. The first theory asserts that the attack was designed simply to test the strength of the Visigothic forces. Another theorizes that the African forces had been dispatched to aid a certain side in the civil war at the time, as their efforts would help build a sound bridge for future alliances and conquests. Others claimed it would have been the first in a string of attacks, prompted by a premeditated invasion to enlarge the Muslim territory. Others believed it was purely an invasion of an exceptionally larger nature, but was one that was unplanned or unmotivated by any "strategic intentions."

A more disturbing cause of attack was found in the 9th century account of the Egyptian Muslim historian, Ibn' Abd al-Hakam. In this account, Julian, the Count of Ceuta and a Christian ruler based in North Africa, approached Tariq ibn Ziyad, the Arab ruler of Morocco, with a stunning proposition. Julian, at this instant a hurting father shaking with unimaginable fury, had supposedly appealed to Ziyad for his assistance in the conquest. Julian accused King Roderic, the tyrannical Visigothic ruler of Spain who had only recently risen to the throne in the year 710, of a heinous crime. Apparently, Roderic, who had been successful in ejecting the previous King Witizza from his throne in a ferocious coup, was not just a ruthless and power-hungry dictator but a sexual predator. Roderic had apparently raped Julian's daughter, and her father, now seeking revenge, wanted nothing more than to "send the Arabs against him."

The same account, the authenticity of which remains in dispute to this day, illustrated how Julian had provided the ships, weapons, and all the necessary equipment to bring the Muslims overseas.

Other accounts suggested that the Jews had played an integral role in the conquest, helping to open the gates and allowing their alleged Muslim collaborators and "liberators" easy entry. Even more compelling, some theorists added that the Jewish people seemed to have no trouble adjusting to life under the new Muslim invaders.

In the year 711, the young and bright-eyed General Ziyad arrived with his massive army of 7,000-10,000 troops. They stepped off their ships and set foot upon what is now known as Gibraltar. This was located on the southern tip of the peninsula, its name derived from its previous moniker, *Jabal At-Tariq*, meaning "Rock of Tariq." Despite the hulking size of Ziyad's forces, his troops set off no alarm bells, as vessels of that size cruising through the straits was a relatively common sight.

Ziyad's army was essentially composed of Arab and Berber soldiers, the latter of which spoke a blend of Afro-Asiatic languages and mostly belonged to the Sunni Muslim faith. As the army sprung forth with their surprise ambush, the defensive troops scrambled into position. This may have been foreign territory, but Ziyad and his men bulldozed right through the city, as the defenses, who had been caught off guard, struggled to stave them off. On the 25th of July in 712, these rumbling conflicts would come to a head in an event now known as the "Battle of Guadalete."

Chroniclers closest to the time period seemed to be in agreement that the number of Roderic's troops had dwarfed Ziyad's. One account even claimed that Roderic had up to 100,000 men in his arsenal, but modern historians have placed the figure closer to 33,000. The defending Visigoth army was split in 2 classes. The first was the noble cavalry, which was well outfitted with sturdy mail armor and glinting weapons that included freshly sharpened swords, axes, lances, and maces that they swung over their heads as they charged forward on horseback. The other class, the Visigoth footmen, made up close to 80% of the army. These were typically the poorer folk of the city, and while they had received adequate training, they lacked sufficient armor and wielded second-rate weapons such as spears, clubs, slings, bows and arrows, and other crude weapons of the like that would be no match to those of Ziyad's men.

Regardless of their numbers, the Visigothic forces were in over their heads, as most of the soldiers' first-hand experience on the field was grossly lacking. The morning of the battle, Ziyad breathed new life into his army with an invigorating speech. Ziyad, who was brimming with confidence, assured them that victory was close at hand. He told his men not to be intimidated by death – if the Grim Reaper should take them, the sooner they would earn the fruits of their rewards in the afterlife. He vowed to fight right alongside them, and promised to have the vicious king Roderic's head.

With adrenaline surging in their systems and Ziyad's words ringing in their ears, the Muslim forces kicked off the final stand. They fended off the Visigothic troops all through mid-morning and soon cast them out with missile fire. Ziyad's winning streak would remain uninterrupted throughout the rest of the day, which resulted in the seriously impaired Visigothic forces backpedaling and regrouping numerous times throughout the battle. Ultimately, as the defensive forces steadily weakened, Ziyad's men managed to surround the Gothic headquarters. It was there, as Ziyad had promised, that he rode into the isolated palace and headed straight for Roderic. The pair faced off in a lengthy scuffle until Ziyad whacked the side of Roderic's helmeted head with his trusty scimitar, sending the Visigothic king flying off his luxurious ruby-studded saddle. Roderic's body crumpled to the ground, disappearing into the chaotic sea of hooves, never to be seen again. An overwhelming number of the Visigothic elite were also said to have been slaughtered by Ziyad's men.

A depiction of Berber cavalry overwhelming the Visigoths during the battle

Left without a leader, what remained of the Visigoths quickly surrendered and skedaddled, seeking refuge in Écija, close to Seville. The Muslims rejoiced in the streets and soon replenished Roderic's throne; from then on, they dominated the Iberian Peninsula, which the new leaders renamed "Al-Andalus." The kingdom experienced another drastic makeover in the new reign that unfolded – the Andalusian Umayyad Dynasty. In the years that followed, the new dynasty entered what is now known as the "Islamic Golden Age."

The Moors haphazardly settled portions of the Iberian Peninsula as they conquered it, but they maintained a heavy population in the region of Cordoba, which they made the center of government. They referred to their new homeland as Al-Andalus, known as Andalusia by Christians.

In the years that followed, the Umayyad dynasty expanded its territory from the Atlantic to the Pyrenees, and while the capital of the Umayyad dynasty lay in Kurtuba, their monumental empire would be divided into 11 realms, which included the Al-Ubushna, Ishbiliya, kadis, Tarif, Balansiyya, Al-mariyya, Gharnatah, and more. It was in this rapidly prospering kingdom that the Islamic Golden Age, a brilliant burst of scientific, cultural, and philosophical advancements, would propel the dynasty forward.

The Islamic Golden Age lasted between the 8th to the mid-13th centuries. The Islamic empire had found a unique way to put itself on the map, as it fostered a multicultural community considered way ahead of its time. It was one of the earliest versions of "universal civilization," as it welcomed a population of "peoples as diverse as the Chinese, the Indians, the people of the Middle East and Africa, black Africans, and white Europeans." This deliberate mingling of cultures activated the rise of a new wave of engineers, scholars, poets, philosophers, geographers, merchants, and other great thinkers. By incorporating ingredients from their North African tradition and merging it with the multifaceted cultures of their newly claimed territory, Moorish Spain was able to make fantastic leaps of advancements in an array of fields such as agriculture, arts, sciences, navigation, philosophy, technology, and more. It soon carved itself a name in the Muslim world as the leading hub for science, education, and business.

One of the most significant and life-changing contributions produced during this period was the pivotal invention of paper. Before then, this sacred recipe was one only the Chinese were privy to, but Muslim authorities were able to extract the intel from war prisoners after the Battle of Talas in 751. The Moors upgraded the invention by altering the recipe to suit their needs, substituting starch in place of the mulberry bark often used by the Chinese. This was helpful because the Moors preferred the use of pens, whereas the Chinese opted for brushes.

The sudden explosion of knowledge, as well as new and improved creations, would eventually find its way to Baghdad and Samarkand. By the year 900, hundreds of public libraries and shops packed with scribes and book-binders had popped up all over Baghdad. It was in this city that the continuously developing knowledge, along with the craft of paper-making, made its way across the seas and into the Moorish kingdom of Spain.

The Spanish-based Moors rolled up their sleeves and went to work immediately, playing an instrumental role of their own in the golden age generated contributions. In the 9th century, inventor Abbas ibn Firnas engineered one of the world's first flying contraptions, centuries before Da Vinci would put pen to paper with his. Firnas' contraption, which was basically a bizarre mechanism with wings and was somewhat reminiscent of a bird costume, though sure to raise some eyebrows today, was applauded by his peers during the time. To the cheers and hollers of the captivated crowd below him, Firnas succeeded in taking off and soaring for a few satisfying seconds before plummeting straight to the ground, partially fracturing his back.

Another notable invention from Moorish Spain during this precious period was the bridge mill, a water mill component of a bridge structure. They would also impart their flavor onto musical instruments – the modern guitar is said to have been inspired by the Arabic *"oud"* instrument, which was later introduced in Medieval Spain as the *"guitarra moresca,"* or in English, the "Moorish guitar." More evidence of the combined cultures can be found in art, literature, and architecture published during the time.

Among the greatest minds that took to the spotlight in Moorish Spain was Abu Zakariya al-

Awwam Ishibili, who pioneered a grafting procedure that would prove pivotal in the surgical world and made waves in the world of botany by singlehandedly naming 500 different species of plants. Another celebrated scholar during this period was Pedro Alfonzo, a Spanish Muslim scientist with a passion for astronomy. Alfonzo had aided in the research of the fledgling science, which he then promoted in the Latin education system. As word of the numerous scientific advancements and triumphs in this region leaked beyond the Al-Andalusian borders, scientists and scholars from across the continent teemed into the kingdom for a dip in the refreshing pool of novel knowledge.

The Moors would also help revitalize the ailing Spanish economy. They founded the silk industry in Al-Andalus and solidified Spain as the center of silk production. The Moors would also dabble in the production of a range of other materials and goods such as cotton, satin, fur, pepper, paper, soaps, maps, and clocks. Under Moorish authority, new libraries, colleges, and public baths were also constructed for the people.

The Moorish presence in Spain has also been praised for the peace and stability brought about by the Umayyad dynasty, Amir Abd al-Rahman I, which lasted roughly from 756-1031. It was Amir who had established the Emirate of Cordoba, which was among the most prestigious of the European territories ruled by a dynastic Islamic monarch. It was also said that Amir had been key in unifying the Muslim leaders strewn across Islamic Europe and convincing them into marrying their powers into one, thereby ruling as a single entity.

Amir Abd al-Rahman I

According to ancient chroniclers, the Muslims, Christians, and Jews in Moorish Spain lived in a society that promoted harmony through religious tolerance. While modern historians agree that some form of tolerance and acceptance was indeed exerted, what had been practiced was in fact an antiquated view of equality. Historian Bernard Lewis best sums up the social status of the non-Muslims in an excerpt from his book, *The Jews of Islam:* "Second class citizenship, though second class, is a kind of citizenship. It involves some rights, though not all...[It is] a recognized status, albeit one of inferiority to the dominant group, which is established by law, recognized by tradition, and confirmed by popular assent, is not to be despised." Generally speaking, non-Muslims of Moorish Spain experienced freedom to a certain extent, so long as they adhered to a special set of rules. While these restrictions and regulations may seem inconceivable today, the non-Muslims were far better off than other prisoners and conquered people of their time. Unlike others who had been browbeaten by abrupt changes in management, the non-Muslims and pagans were not enslaved, nor were they shunned to live in sleazy ghettos. They were not required to convert, nor were they punished, penalized, or executed for their beliefs. They were welcomed in almost every profession, and could contribute as they pleased to the burgeoning culture. While this was the case, most of the non-Muslims pursued less desirable means of income, such as working in butcheries and tanning, but there were also those who chose to work in banking and money-handling.

To identify the non-Muslims and pagans of the area, otherwise known as *"dhimmi"* and *"majus,"* respectively, authorities ensured they sported badges pinned to their chests or sleeves. Construction of new non-Muslim places of worship were either ceased or curbed. *Dhimmi* and *majus* were prohibited from carrying weapons, bequeathing or inheriting any property from Muslims, and employing Muslim slaves. The average non-Muslim or pagan could not appear, provide evidence, or testify in a court of law, and were awarded less compensation for injuries and other matters of the like than their non-dhimmi counterparts. The restrictions even touched on marriage laws; while non-Muslim men were forbidden from tying the knot with Muslim women, a Muslim was free to exchange vows with *dhimmi* or *majus* women if they so wished.

Apart from the rules mentioned above, the *dhimmi* and *majus* were left to their own devices under the following stipulations. First, they were to concede to and fully acknowledge Islamic authority, embracing the superiority of their new leaders. In exchange for their freedom to worship, they, too, were required to remain respectful of the Muslim faith, as well as other religions. They were not to speak ill of any other religion, particularly Islam, and were expected to stay within the boundaries of their own religious circles. Any attempt at conversion to any faith but Islam was entirely out of the question. Finally, they were commanded to cough up a special tax known as the *"jizya"* to Muslim authorities. They were not exempt from any other taxes, and were usually slapped with higher fees and interest rates.

The *dhimmi* and *majus* were not pleased with but could easily make do with these demands. Gradually, they began to indulge themselves with the foreign Muslim culture, and vice versa. Christians who voluntarily learned Arabic, took on Arabic names for themselves, and espoused certain styles of Muslim clothing and customs were referred to as *"Mozarabs."*

Unfortunately, not all of the Moorish rulers were as tolerant. Having risen to the so-called "de facto" throne of Al-Andalus between the late 10th and early 11th centuries, Sultan Almanzor expressed a much more overt contempt for the *dhimmi*. Shortly into his reign, he ordered the looting, torching, and destruction of several of the *dhimmi* churches, and he later tightened the already strict regulations in hopes of further oppressing the non-believers. Christians, in particular, were especially despised by the new Muslim authorities. The new restrictions imposed upon them seemed downright petty. They were no longer allowed to build or live in houses taller than their Muslim neighbors. In the streets, they were required by law to shuffle out of the way for any Muslim that comes across their path. Worse yet, Christians and Jews were barred from displaying any signs of their faith in public. Just the plain act of being spotted with a bible could mean a severe penalty, or even execution.

The animosity against non-Muslims only intensified from there, and the tension came to a head when carnage erupted in the form of a pogrom on December 30, 1066. The Jewish residents of Granada, Spain, fell target to an unanticipated onslaught from a furious Muslim mob. The attackers went on to butcher up to 4,000 of the Jewish inhabitants. Not long after the massacre, the mob captured Joseph Ibn Naghrela, a Jewish vizier who was a high-ranking court official for the Andalusian king. Naghrela flailed, thrashed, and screamed for help, but eventually he was crucified at the hands of his kidnappers.

The mass murder of the Jewish people seemed to have been one of the major contributors to the Moors' dwindling power and authority. As soon as the Christian leaders spotted the multiplying chinks in the Moorish armor, they embarked on a highly productive quest to take back what they deemed was theirs. The *Reconquista* officially began in 718, when the Christian kingdom of Asturias started its first rebellion against the Islamic rulers. Afterwards, several other kingdoms would emerge and unify in attempts to overthrow their Islamic conquerors and develop new Christian rule in the region. Among the kingdoms that led the *Reconquista* were Asturias, León, Castile, Navarre, Aragon, and Portugal, and eventually, they would materialize into two main factions: Castile and Aragon, and Portugal. After a marriage alliance, Castile and Aragon would form Spain.

As with many conflicts throughout history, the straw that broke the camel's back was an increase in the rates of taxation the Christians needed to pay. Emir Anbasa ibn Suhaym Al-Kalbi decided to raise taxes around 718 or 722, which spawned numerous rebellions and riots throughout Al-Andalus. Emir Al-Kalbi lost his position, but the following emirs were unable to stop the rebellions.

Asturias was the first official Christian kingdom to appear on the Iberian Peninsula following the arrival of the caliphate, and Asturias would be the leader of the first forays of the *Reconquista*. Asturias rested in the Cantabrian Mountains on the northern section of the peninsula and managed to resist Muslim conquest because of its wet environment and harsh terrain. A nobleman named Pelayo started the kingdom after returning from the initial Battle of Guadalete against the Muslims in 711.[3] He would be the originator of the Astur-Leonese dynasty and possessed the respect of his people, who had elected him to rule.

After laying the foundations of Asturias, Pelayo dedicated his attention to resisting the rise of the caliphate and driving the invaders back out of the peninsula. He created his capital in Cangas de Onís, secured his territory, ensured he possessed few rivals, and then plotted his next steps.

---

[3] Roger Collins, *The Arab Conquest of Spain 710-797*, (Hoboken: Blackwell Publishing, 1989), pg. 49.

The next kingdom to emerge was Basque Navarre, another Christian territory close to Asturias. Although small, it maintained its independence because it was on the other side of the Pyrenees Mountains and out of the way of the Umayyads. Realizing it would be madness to try to attack the Christian kingdoms in such unfavorable terrain, the Umayyad rulers instead focused on consolidating their power in mainland Iberia and mostly ignored Asturias and Navarre. Occasionally, military forces made up of a combination of Berbers and Arabs would attempt to cross the mountains, but there was little interest from the administration in trying to take territory. With this in mind, it can be said that the original Christian kingdoms were successful in founding the *Reconquista* and keeping it alive simply because the Umayyad Caliphate had no interest in fighting and did not see Asturias and Navarre as a threat.

As for the Christian kingdoms, they did not have much reason to attack the caliphate. Alphonse I of Asturias also knew it would be suicide to attempt to cross the Pyrenees and focused instead on attacking Arab-Berber strongholds in the mountains and on expanding his own territory by attacking nearby Christian territories that had managed to hold out against the caliphate. Among his targets were the neighboring Basque and Galicia. He was not always successful, there was a new movement of Christian kingdoms determined to restore the power of the Visigoths. The kings of Asturias considered themselves the successors of the original monarchy in Toledo, which had been overthrown upon the death of Roderic. With that in mind, they justified their decision to expand to southern Iberia.

Despite such lofty claims, Asturias and the following Christian kingdoms possessed few similarities to the original Visigoths, but regardless, the decision to push south constituted the beginning of the *Reconquista*.

A monument to Pelayo

Although there were obviously some religious tensions between Christians and Muslims, the initial fighting during the *Reconquista* was not religious in nature as much as it was another power grab by yet another new monarchy in the medieval world. This trend would continue for at least another century until religious differences started to color the interactions, rebellions, and wars between the Christian kingdoms and the Muslim caliphate. Moreover, when the *Reconquista* started, it was not a cohesive effort; Asturias was originally not much of a kingdom, consisting primarily of refugees and guerrilla fighters who had been resisting the expansion of the caliphate.

The Muslim Invasion of France

While they were in the process of conquering the Iberian Peninsula, the Moors came into contact with the Franks, and they did so at a time when the lawfully recognised king essentially had no power. The real power was exercised by an official called the Mayor of the Palace, the steward of the royal household. He held power over a realm that extended from the Duchy of Aquitaine in southern Gaul to Brittany in the west, the Rhine in the north, and the Bavarian border. As noted above, while Hispania was being invaded, Francia was beset with civil war following the death of King Pepin II in 714, but by 718 the realm had been reunited under the Mayor of the Palace Charles Martel, acting in the name of King Chilperic II. Even if the Franks had been in a position to help the Visigoths against the Umayyads at the time, it is doubtful that they would have done so, as the Visigoths had formerly ruled Aquitaine and remained rivals for influence in southern Gaul. Moreover, the Franks eyed the Visigothic presence in Septimania with envy.

Septimania, which bordered both the Kingdom of Francia and the Frank-dominated Duchy of Aquitaine, was the last province of the Visigoths to fall to the Moors, and a brief description of the province is important because it featured prominently in the war between the Moors and the Franks. As a political entity it no longer exists, but it occupied the coastal region of France between the Pyrenees and the River Rhone and included the towns of Narbonne, Bezier and Carcassone. The highlands of the Massif Central form its northern border. The Romans named it after the Seventh Legion stationed there, though the Visigoths always called it Gallia (Gaul), a contraction of Gallia Narbonnensis. The people of Septimania were referred to as Gauls by the Goths and spoke a vulgarized form of Latin. The region was ruled by a Gothic duke and aristocracy who were despised by the populace. Pockets of paganism survived into the 8th century as attested by the survival of the practice of not working on Thursdays in honor of Jupiter.[4] Many of the Christians differed from their Catholic countrymen in that they did not believe that Jesus Christ was God, a relic of the Germanic embrace of Arianism.

For a time, the Visigothic kings of Iberia favoured Narbonne as their capital but frequent conflicts with the Franks over the province eventually dissuaded them. It was prized as a particularly rich province, with the climate then (as now) favoring agricultural produce, including wine. Narbonne and other towns were important trading centers with other Mediterranean ports, including Rome, Palermo, Venice and Constantinople. They also traded with the Franks along the Rhone Valley and with the cities of Iberia, thus obviating the need to cross the difficult and treacherous passes of the Pyrenees. The towns of Septimania may then be imagined as vibrant, prosperous,s and probably cosmopolitan communities in which a variety of merchants from various countries and their goods could be found.

As the Moors overran Iberia, much of the Visigothic nobility fled to Septimania and there elected Ardo, the last of the Visigothic kings. The Moors pursued them and from 719-720 devastated the land. In 720, Narbonne was captured and the Moors offered its inhabitants generous terms. From there they methodically captured the towns and fortresses that still held

---

[4] McKenna, Stephen (1938). *Paganism and Pagan Survivals in Spain up to the Fall of the Visigothic Kingdom*. Catholic University of America Press.

out. As in Andalusia the inhabitants of the province were not obliged to convert to Islam, but many did so for reasons of social advantage. The fate of Ardo is unclear - he may have perished in defense of his realm or negotiated a treaty which allowed him to live in Andalusia.[5]

In the wake of that, the Moors headed toward Aquitaine, nominally a vassal of the Frankish king but in effect an independent state. Its duke, Odo the Great, had gained recognition of autonomy from Charles Martel in exchange for surrendering the hapless Chilperic II. Like Septimania, Aquitaine was prosperous and appealed to Moorish raiders eager for booty and slaves. The Arab and Berber nobility were not tied to the lands - they were nomads and lived largely on plunder and trade, particularly trade in slaves. Under Islamic law, non-Muslims could be despoiled of their goods and enslaved, so the prospect of plundering Aquitaine and Francia was not only attractive but a necessity.

At first the incursion into Aquitaine was halted by an alliance between Odo and Manuza (not to be confused with the commander who fought Pelagius), the disgruntled Berber governor of Catalonia in northeast Hispania. Munuza was quickly defeated and when the governor of Andalusia, Al-Samh ibn Malik al-Khawlani, headed toward Odo's capital Toulouse the duke crossed into Francia to seek help from the Franks. In his absence the Umayyads laid siege to the town.

Charles Martel did not commit to assisting his vassal, preferring to see what advantage he might take from the situation, so Odo was left to recruit an army himself. After three months Odo returned with a force of Franks (probably Franks settled in Aquitaine), Aquitainians, and Gascons, and he managed to surprise the Moors at the Battle of Toulouse on June 9, 721. They had not expected the duke to return, and Al-Samh hoped that Toulouse would fall quickly, so he concentrated on forcing its surrender.

When the Moorish general discovered that Odo and his army was almost upon them, he swung his cavalry to meet it. Given the haste with which Odo raised a force, his numbers could not have been great, nor perhaps the same quality of the Moors. His army probably consisted of a core of heavy infantry with militia levies along with some cavalry. The Andalusian troops in contrast were mostly fast hard-hitting cavalry and veterans of the Visigoth campaigns.

For a time, it seemed that the Aquitainian lines would break, but Odo withdrew before they did, predicting that Al-Samh would not withdraw but return to the siege. In this he was proved correct, and as the Aquitainian forces were observed marching away the Moors moved back toward Toulouse to settle down for the night. The beleaguered garrison was incapable of sallying forth and Odo was in retreat, so the Moors neglected to post watchmen or erect fortifications in the camp. This was to prove a fatal mistake, for under cover of darkness Odo's army marched

---

[5] Collins, Roger.(1989) *The Arab Conquest of Spain, 710–97*. Blackwell Publishing, p.45.

back toward Toulouse. Before dawn, the Aquitainians fell upon the Moors, and Al-Samh was too late in the attempt to rally his troops. They were trapped between Odo and Toulouse with nowhere to flee, and what followed was not so much a battle as a massacre, as most of the Moors were slaughtered within a few minutes. Al-Samh escaped, mortally wounded, to Narbonne, where he died, and with that, the Moorish invasion of Western Europe had been checked for the first time in a decade.

Odo proudly boasted in a letter to Pope Gregory II that his troops killed 375,000, but this is clearly typical of the medieval tendency to exaggerate battle numbers[6] and probably represented the duke's opinion of the decisiveness of the victory. Regardless, the pope showered Odo with gifts and proclaimed him the savior of Christendom. A legend arose that three baskets of bread had been blessed by Gregory and sent to the Franks before the battle, and that when Odo distributed the bread to his troops, nobody who ate it died or was wounded.

In reality, the disaster at Toulouse only temporarily halted the Moors' incursion into Gaul, but it did have the effect of protecting Odo from Charles Martel, who could not be seen to be attacking the hero who had saved Gaul. Charles could nevertheless use it to his own advantage, for he had time to prepare for a conflict with the Muslims that he must have known was inevitable.

Around the same time as the Battle of Toulouse in 721, Moorish forces suffered another defeat at the hands of Visigothic noblemen who had fled to the nearly inaccessible Cantabrian Mountains on the North Coast in the region known as Asturias. This encounter influenced future events because it opened a front against the Moors which diverted troops and resources from Gaul and later aided Charlemagne in his invasion of Hispania. After the stinging defeat of Toulouse, the Moorish governor of Andalusia, Anbasa, resolved to bolster morale by conquering Asturias, which had never fully succumbed to Moorish domination. The rebels, both Visigoths and indigenous Asturians, were led by Pelagius, traditionally regarded as the first king of Asturias, though in reality he was probably simply one of the more powerful warlords. He probably faced the Moors' invasion in 722 with just a few hundred men, but he and his followers possessed an enormous advantage thanks to the mountainous geography and the fact that there were no roads. Both the terrain and the lack of roads hindered the Moors, who relied heavily on cavalry, and Pelagius withdrew his forces to a narrow valley near the village of Covadonga.

After demanding Pelagius's surrender, the Moors' commander, Alkama, led his crack troops through the constricted valley, probably aware of the danger he was entering. Sure enough, the Asturians on the valley ridge began firing arrows and dropping stones on the Moors, who were unable to flee or find shelter. With the Moorish troops in confusion, Pelagius and his troops suddenly appeared from the caves and rocks of the valley walls and set upon the enemy. Almost

---

[6] Nelson, Janet L. (2019). *King and Emperor: A New Life of Charlemagne*. Oakland, California: University of California Press, p.32.

all of the Moors were slaughtered, with only a handful escaping. Pelagius went on to rout another army commanded by the general Munuza in similar circumstances.

As discomforting as these defeats were for the Moors, their raiding into Aquitaine resumed, albeit without the intention of seizing the major strongholds. From Septimania, the Moors also raided along the Rhone Valley and plundered Burgundy for more than 300 miles, as far as Langres and Sens.

However, back in Andalusia further troubles were brewing. The Berber partners of the Arab conquerors had long been dissatisfied with the partnership. The Arabs tended to give their Berber partners the poorer shares of land and booty while simultaneously giving them the most onerous duties. Moreover, they imposed higher taxes on the Berbers than on other Muslim subjects and exacted slave tributes from them. The Umayyad Caliph had forbidden these deprivations, but the governors of Andalusia, far away from the capital in Damascus and left to their own desires, needed money, and discrimination against the Berbers made these exactions easier. In truth the Arabs regarded the Berbers as recent converts (northwest Africa had been conquered by the Umayyads less than a century earlier) and only half-hearted Muslims.

As a result of the tensions, sporadic revolts break out in Andalusia, which were put down with difficulty, and since the Arab masters of Hispania struggled to maintain cohesion, defeats on the battlefield allowed the Berbers to point to the incompetence of their lords, which only compounded the difficulties. A great victory was needed, and booty was needed so that taxes and public unrest might be alleviated.

This was no doubt a powerful incentive to risk a larger and more daring expedition into Aquitaine and Francia, and in 732 the governor of Andalusia, Abdul Rahman, decided to gather a force that would pillage its way through Aquitaine into the very heartland of Francia itself. It was unquestionably a daring move since he genuinely had no idea of what kind of resistance he would encounter.

When word of the Muslim force's campaign reached Odo the Great, he fled Toulouse with whatever forces he could muster and reported to the court of Charles Martel. On this occasion, Martel was sufficiently concerned to summon his nobles and assemble an army.

Though he was essentially the leader of Francia at the time, Charles Martel was born the illegitimate son of the Mayor of the Palace, Pepin of Heristal, and his concubine Alpaida.[7] Martel's age at the time of the Battle of Tours is uncertain, but it was probably between 42 and 58.[8] He had been Mayor of the Palace since 718, succeeding his uncle and Pepin's grandson,

---

[7] Though nominally Chriatians the Frankish puppet-kings often kept concubines in the manner of their pagan predecessors.

[8] Charles S. Peirce (7 December 2009). *Writings of Charles S. Peirce: A Chronological Edition*. **8**. Peirce Edition Project. p. 441

Theudoald. Martel was not his name, but an honorific meaning "hammer" in Old French, referring to his defeat of the Moors. European history has exalted him as the savior of Western Christendom and the founder of a new dynasty of Frankish kings, the Carolingians (from the Latin word "Carolus," meaning "Charles"), though it was his son Pepin III who was the first king of that line.

The actual king in the year of the Battle of Tours was Theuderic IV, who was kept in honorable captivity at the old Roman town of Otmus, which according to tradition changed its name to Château-Thierry (Thierry being the French name for Theuderic). As mentioned before, the King of the Franks had been reduced to a ceremonial role, but Theuderic IV's position gave legitimacy to the government and ensured the sanction of the Church, since it was the king, not the Mayor, who was anointed with sacred oil and crowned by the Bishop of Reims. He was far too valuable a person to be allowed to move freely, which was why he was respectfully confined.

Like Hispania before the arrival of the Moors, Francia essentially remained a Roman province governed by a layer of Germanic nobility. The Franks governed themselves according to Germanic law, but the people observed Roman law and customs and spoke a form of vulgar Latin which in time became French. That is not to say that the aristocracy did not adopt certain Roman traditions as well, as they considered themselves the successors of the Roman governors and patricians they supplanted. They maintained such military and administrative titles as duke (*dux*) and count (*comes*) and adopted elements of Roman style in their dress and court ceremonies. They adopted the Roman religion, Christianity, and liberally endowed the churches and monasteries of the kingdom and appointed the bishops. Like the Byzantine emperors in Constantinople, the lords of the Franks assumed certain rights over the Church, but church officials in Francia looked for guidance to the pope.

The Franks also continued and augmented Roman roads, fortifications, and city walls, which stabilized the kingdom and encouraged trade. This was necessary because the Frankish realm was plagued not only by the Moors, but by the Saxons in the north, Lombards in Italy, and Slavs on the eastern frontier. The Franks also maintained the tradition of a standing army, maintained by the Mayor of the Palace and the greater magnates. The king had his own personal army, the elite *scarae*, and the Mayor of the Palace could also issue the Ban *(Bannum)*, by which royal officials were empowered to levy troops from the general populace. Failure to comply would result in a hefty fine and possibly death.

The core of the Frankish army was still the infantry since the age of the heavily armored knight was yet to come. Charles Martel did raise a cavalry force, but it was not equipped for head-on charges. Instead, they were used as a mobile force that could raid, ambush, and attack isolated formations. Aquitainian troops in particular were renowned for their prowess with javelins, while Frankish cavalry were armed with scale-mail, helmets, shields, swords, and spears, very much like the cavalry of the Roman Empire near its collapse. Such equipment was expensive, so only members of the aristocracy served as cavalrymen. Frankish cavalry did not use stirrups, so they may have fought on foot for much of the time.

The infantry consisted of heavy units drawn from the wealthier gentry and the lightly armored or unarmored militia. At the time of the Battle of Tours, the infantry was probably still using axes, though that weapon was being phased out in favor of spears since the latter were more effective against cavalry. They only sometimes made use of bows, and like the cavalry, the infantry differed little from their Roman counterparts. This is hardly surprising given that the Romans relied heavily on Germanic mercenaries as the Western Roman Empire was collapsing in the late 5th century.

The army that the Franks would confront had the backing of Europe's strongest empire since the collapse of Rome. It consisted primarily of Arab and Berber light to medium cavalry armed with helmet, shield, chain or scale mail, lance and sword. They employed few mounted archers. There was probably not a large infantry contingent, given that the Moors used foot soldiers for support and for sieges, and the Moorish army in Gaul bypassed the major fortresses. If the purpose of the invasion was plunder – as seems likely – light and medium cavalry would serve the purpose better.

The Moors seemed to know very little about the country they were invading. They were dressed and equipped for a warm, dry autumn rather than the typically cool and wet climate of central France, which would have afflicted the soldiers and hampered the movement of supplies.

The commander, Abdul Rahman, was an Arab who had served in the Umayyad administration of the Mahgreb in northwest Africa. He was present at the Battle of Toulouse and in 730 was appointed ruler of all Andalusia by Caliph Hisham ibn Abd al-Malik. He was an intelligent administrator of considerable talent and wisdom, which has led many to wonder why he was leading an expedition into unknown territory against a foe of which he knew little. He may have been under the impression that the Franks were ineffective barbarian rulers who would collapse as the Visigoths had. In fact, the Moors still knew little about Germanic kingdoms even after the invasion of Hispania, which had only occurred two decades before. Most of their experience of Christian armies had been with the advanced and sophisticated Byzantines, and they probably regarded Westerners as tribal, fractured, and barbaric. The attraction of booty and slaves was tempting, as the Franks were generous patrons of the Church, and richly-endowed monasteries and churches proliferated, especially in the region of Tours. The Abbey of Saint Martin in Tours itself was particularly wealthy.

Whatever the purpose of the invasion, Abdul Rahman and his main force was headed toward Tours by the beginning of October 732, and Tours was one of the most important cities in Gaul. As Civitas Turonum, it was the capital of the Roman province of Lugdunum and protected the important trade routes along the Loire. A 4th century bishop of the city, Martin of Tours, was widely venerated as a saint throughout Western Europe, and Tours became a site of pilgrimage and commerce. It's apparent that Tours was the intended destination of the Moorish army, and though the battle has taken its name, it is unclear whether Tours was the actual location of the climactic confrontation. The battle is often named after Poitiers (Pictavium for the Franks), a city about 65 miles south-south west of Tours, and it probably occurred somewhere between the two. After the famous Battle of Poitiers was fought in 1356 between the French and English, it became more convenient to name the 732 battle after Tours.

One contemporary source from the Frankish perspective concerning the Battle of Tours is *History of the Lombards* by Paul the Deacon. Paul was a Benedictine monk associated with the royal court of the Lombards, who were, like the Franks and Visigoths, Germanic. They ruled most of Italy at the time, and Paul wrote his account about 60 years after the battle. As the name of the work suggests, it was concerned primarily with the history of his own people, so the history of the Franks that he related was focused on how it affected the Lombards, and much of what he wrote about Tours is simply impossible. For example, he claimed 375,000 Moors were slain when the largest force fielded by the Umayyads had about 120,000 soldiers (at the 717 Siege of Constantinople).[9] Medieval chroniclers were notorious for exaggerating battle statistics, and unlike modern historians they were principally interested in writing narratives rather than analytical texts. As such, they were given to hyperbole, especially when their accounts had propaganda value.

At the same time, Arab accounts tend to diminish the importance of the encounters with the Franks and are more concerned with civil war between the Berbers and Arabs in Andalusia. The Arab sources tended to see this as the main cause of the subsequent decline of the Umayyad dynasty rather than the Battle of Tours.

That said, both Arab and Western sources agree that the battle occurred and agree on the basic facts. Details must be drawn from historical knowledge of the opposing armies and their battle tactics, and inferences might reasonably be made.

It seems clear that Abdul Rahman neglected to send scouts ahead to Tours, evidently confident that there was no army large enough to challenge him nearby. If he had learned that Martel had been fighting the Saxons in the north, that may have been a reasonable expectation, though one wonders why he did not wish to know the terrain and conditions ahead. It is possible that his army was already carrying so much loot that no advance force could be spared.

As it turned out, Martel, fresh from victories over the Saxons, was directly in the Moors' path. His presence was detected around October 3, and the Franks did not immediately attack. The Moors were not keen to engage either, seemingly slowed by the vast quantity of treasure they had already pillaged and not yet at full strength. Instead, the two sides engaged in skirmishes for

---

[9] Greek, Eric E. (2019). "The Myth of Charles Martel: Why the Islamic Caliphate Ceased Military Operations in Western Europe After the Battle of Tours," Master's thesis, Harvard Extension School, p.23.

the next seven days.

Abdul Rahman was furious that he had allowed Martel to choose his position. The Franks were encamped on a hill behind a forest, masking their true size, but Martel probably commanded only about 20,000 men and was likely outnumbered by the Moors. The alternative to attacking was to retreat, but the Moorish soldiers likely would not have wanted to abandon the chance of sacking Tours.

By October 10, the troops bringing up the booty had arrived and Rahman had to make a decision. The cold was beginning to affect the lightly dressed Moorish troops, who could not remain in Gaul during the winter. He knew Martel would not break his own formation to attack, and that the Franks could receive supplies from Tours, whereas his own troops were running out of food and the local harvest had finished. Ultimately, Rahman made up his mind to attack.

Conversely, Martel had studied the enemy well and had drawn his army into a phalanx formation (rectangular blocks with spears at the ready on all sides). At the time, and for several centuries to come, cavalry were the best shock troops to break formations, but on this occasion successive Moorish charges failed to move the tightly packed Frankish infantry. The Moors were charging uphill and thus lost most of their impetus by the time they made contact. Rahman hoped the Franks would pursue the retreating cavalry into the open field, where his troops would have the advantage, but the Franks maintained discipline, remaining, as one chronicler put it, "immobile as a wall."[10] Rahman hoped to reach Martel himself, despite not knowing what he looked like, and at one point his cavalry appeared to penetrate the Frankish lines. Any hope was short-lived, however, as this assault was driven back like the others.

By now the Moors were exhausted, but they continued their attacks. The alternative was withdrawal, and the temptation of plunder in Tours must have been great. It was at this point, when the Moors were most vulnerable, that Duke Odo took a force of his Aquitainians held in reserve (probably in the forest where they would have been unobserved), swept past the Moorish flanks, and attacked their camp. He freed captives intended for slavery and seized plunder, prompting many of the Moors to race back in defense of their gains. Abdul Rahman, at the head of his troops, attempted to stop the chaotic withdrawal, and while most soldiers stayed in place, disorder had already infected the ranks. Charles then ordered his outer units to attack the flanks, while he led the center in a counter-charge. The Moors were surrounded and slaughtered, and Rahman perished with his men.

---

[10] Anonymous, *The Mozarabic Chronicle of 754.*

The Battle of Tours as depicted in the *Grandes Chroniques de France*

As the Moors withdrew, the Franks did not pursue the survivors, and Odo returned to his position with Charles. Martel was probably wise to be cautious, because sending his infantry forward in an open field would make them vulnerable to the swifter cavalry. He therefore remained in his position, resting his troops and tending to the dead and wounded, while the Moors retired toward what remained of their camp.

The following day, the Franks expected another wave of attacks, given that the Moors had been mauled but not destroyed. When no attack came, scouts were sent forth, and they reported that the enemy camp was abandoned. The Moors' losses are difficult to ascertain and contemporary reports are notoriously unreliable, but it would be fair to assume they lost half of their army and Frankish losses would have been small by comparison. Still, the remaining force would likely have matched that of the Franks in terms of numbers.

Even if the two sides were now at equal strength in manpower, the Moors fully understood that the Franks would not shift from his position blocking the road to Tours. The temperature was dropping and the army was lacking food and water. The surviving leaders therefore decided to return to Al-Andalusia.

The retreat home could not have been easy. In their haste to reach Tours, the Moors had bypassed strategic strongholds in Francia and Aquitaine, which subsequently harassed the retreating troops. At the same time, the Moorish cavalry may have sacked some towns and villages on the way back.

Abdul-Malik ibn Katan al-Fihri, the 15th Umayyad governor of Al-Andalusia and Abdul Rahman's successor, was forced to deal with the aftermath of the disaster at Tours. Fortunately for him, Charles Martel had no plans to invade, as he was more interested in conquering Aquitaine from Odo the Great. A small band of Aquitainians did seize Pamplona, however, and Malik's failure to defeat them or the Christian Basques in the Pyrenees led to his deposition and imprisonment by Uqba ibn al-Hajjaj, who became the new governor in 734. It was around this time that Berber unrest began to intensify again.

Nevertheless, the Moors felt sufficiently secure to dispatch a new army into Gaul, this time from Septimania. It would march out from Narbonne and seize the city of Avignon, which, positioned on the left bank of the Rhone in Provence, would prove a secure base for pillaging the heart of the Frankish realm. The fortress surrendered in 734, and this time the Moors made sure that scouts were sent forth to ascertain the location of Frankish forces. Uqba also made alliances with some of the lords of Aquitaine.

At the time, Charles was preoccupied with affairs in Aquitaine. Odo had fallen from power and the Frankish Mayor wished to force Aquitaine to submit to him. It is unclear if Odo died in 735 or was deposed or entered a monastery, but whatever his fate he exited the scene, and after Martel seized Bordeaux in 735, Odo's son and successor, Hunald, acknowledged the overlordship of King Theuderic IV. However, Hunald led a revolt the following year, and during that war, Hunald and his brother Hatto were defeated, with the latter imprisoned. When he escaped, his own brother pursued him, blinded him, and incarcerated him in a monastery to secure peace with Charles. Charles was content to allow Hunald to remain his vassal rather than seize his territory, and he was now free to move against the Moors raiding the Rhone Valley from Avignon.

When Martel advanced toward Avignon, the Moors withdrew to the city with no hope of immediate reinforcement, for the magnates who had opposed Odo now swore allegiance to Hunald and Charles. From Avignon, the Moors hoped to use the Franks' own engineering prowess against the Moors. At a time when most Westerners still used hill fortifications surrounded by wooden palisades, the Franks constructed impressive structures of stone. Their ability to fortify positions had in fact allowed them to build their extensive empire, and they were even capable of diverting rivers to defend positions. In contrast, the Umayyads, who relied on large numbers of cavalry to cover vast amounts of territory rapidly, were not suited to siege warfare, so they were only too happy to rely on the Franks' own defenses while they held Avignon.

Despite their best efforts, the Moors found themselves surprised yet again, for the army of

Charles far outnumbered their own. The Mayor of the Palace brought ballistae, catapults, battering rams, and scaling ladders, and in 737 they stormed the city. Ironically, after the Franks captured Avignon, they destroyed it as punishment for surrendering to the Moors.

Martel could now march on to Narbonne, but the Moors were not defenseless. They could call on troops from Andalusia, who would not be hampered by the Pyrenees, or reinforcements could sail directly into the ports of Septimania and Provence. Provence was a duchy nominally subject to the Frankish kings, but in practice it was governed by the ancient Gallo-Roman aristocracy. None of the Germanic tribes had effectively settled there, despite it being ruled by Visigoths, Ostrogoths, and Burgundians successively. Arabs and Berbers from the Umayyad Caliphate had also tried to settle there, but they were unable to do so permanently. Like the Aquitainians, the nobles of Provence hoped to throw off the yolk of Charles Martel, and it was their duke Maurontus who had given Avignon to the Moors and requested the help of Yusuf ibn Abdul-Rahman, Umayyad governor of Septimania. The Moors also had forces near the coastal city of Arles, which commanded the mouth of the Rhone.

In 737, Charles Martel, with his brother Duke Childebrand of Burgundy, was ready to continue his advance toward Narbonne. Narbonne was a prosperous port and appropriately fortified, so it posed a formidable challenge to the Franks. While they besieged it, the Franks learned that a substantial relief force was arriving by sea, so Martel sent the greater part of his army to meet the reinforcements about 10 miles to the south at the River Berre. The Moorish army was smashed and sent fleeing back to the boats. Amongst the casualties was their commander, Omar-ibn-Chaled, and many survivors were speared as they floundered in the shallows.

The Battle of the River Berre was arguably as important as the Battle of Tours, yet it remains virtually unknown and details about the fighting are scant. In 732, it was doubtful that the Moors wished to invade Gaul with the intention of establishing permanent bases, but the threat they posed five years later was greater, for the fortresses of Septimania and Provence did give them bases from which they could launch comprehensive conquests of Frankish territory. The defeat of the Moorish reinforcements was therefore a decisive nettle.

The Berre is a tributary of the Aude, which begins in the Pyrenees and empties into the Mediterranean near Narbonne. The battle was fought on swamp ground between the river and sea, from which the Moors had come. Indeed, the fleet of vessels that transported them from Andalusia was still present when the Franks arrived. The Moors were surprised and limited by their geography, with the river to the west, the sea to the east, and the marsh surrounding them. They were routed and fled toward the nearby lagoons, where their ships were moored. Many were cut down, and many prisoners and treasures were taken.

Despite the victory, Martel realized that he could not assault Narbonne given his own losses. Furthermore, Duke Hunald of Aquitaine had broken his oath of fealty and threatened his freedom of movement. He therefore contented himself with sacking the strongholds of Septimania, including Nimes, Agde, and Beziers. Martel did aim to expel the Moors from their bases in neighboring Provence and to punish its duke, Maurontus, but for the moment the strength of the Provencal fortresses defied him. He therefore made an alliance with Luitprand, King of the Lombards, who ruled much of Italy, and with his help the Franks savaged the towns of Provence. Massalia (Marseilles), Aix-en-Provence, Toulon, and other settlements.

By 739, Charles was in command of the region and Maurontus was fleeing across the Alps. The Moorish strongholds were destroyed and their former masters in Andalusia judged it foolhardy to attempt to take them back. Charles appointed a Burgundian nobleman, Abbo, to rule the duchy in his name, after which he withdrew to Paris to attend to various affairs of state that he had sidelined for five years. For the time being, he had to leave Narbonne in the hands of the Moors, figuring they were too weak to be anything more than a nuisance.

After these defeats, the Berbers, already alienated by their Arab masters, revolted against them. The uprising began in Tangiers in 740 and was an immediate response to an Arab declaration that the Berbers were conquered peoples and would be treated as such. Their conversion to Islam was relatively recent, and the Arabs regarded them as little more than heathens, so much so that they imposed on them the *dhimmi* tax, which by Islamic law was only paid by non-Muslim subjects. The Umayyads had suffered a crippling loss of revenue and trade in slaves since Charles Martel thwarted their expeditions into Gaul, and they came to see the Berber population as a possible source to offset the losses. The reversals in Septimania and Provence factored into the revolt, which swiftly spread to Andalusia where the Arabs were greatly outnumbered, and the withdrawal of Arab garrisons in the north of the country to deal with the Berbers encouraged the Visigothic refugees in Asturias to strike out from their mountainous strongholds. Their king, Alphonse I, commanded expeditions that conquered Galicia in northwest Hispania and territory to the south to the Ebro River.

The Arab forces proved incapable of holding back the Berbers, and in desperation the governor Yusuf called in Syrian troops, who became as difficult to control as the Berbers. Civil war broke out between the Andalusian Arabs and the Syrians, and it was not until 743 that a semblance of order was restored. By then, the stability of Andalusia had greatly suffered, and Syrian warlords now ruled the provinces in an autonomous fashion. Indeed, the central government in Cordoba never really recovered its authority, and the Berbers of Mahgreb had managed to overthrow the Umayyads and establish their own states. Andalusia was now separated from the rest of the Umayyad Caliphate by land.

Worse was to come. Shortly after the Berber revolt, the Abbasid dynasty of Khorasan (north-east Iran) also rebelled against the Umayyads and by 750 had conquered the entire caliphate. The Fihrids, the ruling Arab family of Andalusia, come to prominence during the civil war when the Abbasid Caliph Abu Abbass refused to recognize Andalusian autonomy.

Historically, the Islamic invasion of France has not attracted as much popular attention as the

Ottoman campaigns in Eastern Europe, perhaps because the invasion of Europe from North Africa in the 8th century was not viewed as posing the same threat. There are historians who believe that the Umayyads never intended to settle the Iberian Peninsula or conquer parts of France, and in that vein, some have argued that the Battle of Tours was inconsequential altogether. In *The Reader's Companion to Military History*, Robert Cowley and Geoffrey Parker asserted that "several of the battles that Edward Shepherd Creasy listed in his famous 1851 book *The Fifteen Decisive Battles of the World* rate hardly a mention here, and the confrontation between Muslims and Christians at Poitiers-Tours in 732, once considered a watershed event, has been downgraded to a raid in force."

Other authors point to the rapid succession of conquests enjoyed by the Umayyad Caliphate in a relatively short period of time and consider Tours a mere anomaly. The Umayyads needed only a few years to conquer Hispania, and it took the Christians 700 years to complete the *Reconquista*. Some have further pointed out that the defeat of the Andalusian incursion at Septimania, which bore the characteristics of an actual invasion, was far more decisive than Tours in ensuring that Europe remained Christian north of the Pyrenees.

That said, there are still traces of the Moors' presence in Gascony, Aquitaine, and Provence to this day. The Provencal word for "translator," *drogoman*, comes from the Arabic *tordjman*. The word *charabia*, "to discuss," is borrowed from the Arabic *charaha*. The little town of Ramatuelle, nestled in the hills near St.Tropez, was a Moorish settlement originally called Rahmatollah ("the mercy of God").

While the Moors might never have been strong enough to consolidate control of France, the outcome of Tours played a massive role on Frankish history and the direction in which Europe was shaped by Charlemagne. If Martel had lost the battle or had been killed there, a civil war likely would have ensued, rendering the Franks more vulnerable to future invasions. Furthermore, even if the Franks were not replaced by Muslims, their ties to Catholicism ensured Western Europe would be dominated by Catholics for the next 800 years, and had they been replaced by other local groups in France, that might not have happened. Large sections of society clung to pagan traditions, and the Frankish kings themselves continued to keep concubines. A number of Frankish bishops, such as Gaugericus, complained that heathenism continued to flourish amongst their people.[11] Islam might easily have taken root in less Christianized regions, or other forms of Christianity might have.

The Emirate of Cordoba

The fall of the Umayyad Caliphate in the 740s brought more troubles to Andalusia. In 756 Abdul Rahman, leader of the Arab Fihrid family, proclaimed himself Emir at Cordoba, but he

---

[11] Butler, Alban. "Saint Gery, or Gaugericus, Bishop and Confessor." *Lives of the Fathers, Martyrs, and Principal Saints, 1866*

struggled to exert real control over the Syrian fiefdoms and both the Franks and the Asturians took advantage of his weakness to make gains. After a dispute with the new Abbasid caliph, Rahman foolishly invited an exiled Umayyad prince onto Andalusian shores. This was another Abdul Rahman, and he set his standard in Andalusian soil as the rightful Emir of Cordoba. In the civil war that followed, the Fihrid princes, probably in desperation, sent envoys to Charles the Great (Charlemagne), King of the Franks. They told Charles that the emirs of Catalonia and Saragossa would submit to him as his vassals and march with his armies in return for military aid against the Umayyads. Charles agreed. He wanted a buffer zone against Andalusia and may have thought he might even conquer all of it. In 778, he led a two-pronged invasion across the Pyrenees. One army reached friendly Barcelona while Charles himself made for Pamplona, which fell relatively easily. Charles directed that the two armies meet at Saragossa, held by Husayn, the Fihrid emir, and from there they would drive south, but Husayn changed his mind and refused Charles entry. The siege that followed stalled the campaign to detrimental effect. The Saragossans offered Charles gold, which the king, learning of an uprising in Saxony, accepted and his army withdrew to Pamplona.

Pamplona was the principal stronghold of the Basque peoples, who preferred the rule of the Moors who tended to leave them be rather than that of the Franks or of the Asturians who attempted to dominate them. Charles suspected that they would rebel as soon as he returned to Gaul and so leveled Pamplona to the ground together with several towns and villages. The infuriated Basques pursued his army and set upon it in a narrow pass, near Roncesvalles, on August 15, 778. The Frankish rearguard was slaughtered, almost to a man, but Charles escaped. The most famous of the warriors to fall was Roland, the governor of the Breton Marc. In the romanticized *Song of Roland*, composed in the 11th century, he is a nephew of Charles and is borne away by angels after a heroic death.

Charles left garrisons throughout the territories he conquered and the embattled Moors – Fihrid or Umayyad - were in no position to recover them. Charles was however dealt something of a blow, and never again ventured into Andalusia. Yet his generals in the Hispanic March continued to extend their influence southward. The County of Barcelona was entirely conquered by 802 and the County of Aragon was established around the same time. The humiliation of Roncesvalles was at length revenged and the Basques conquered, and the Franks gave assistance to the Kingdom of Asturias, thus strengthening that state's hold on the Moorish territory.

One of the border marches established by Charlemagne still exists as the Principality of Andorra. The National Anthem of Andorra, *El Gran Carlemany*, contains the following verse:

"The great Charlemagne, my father

From the Arabs liberated me

And from heaven gave me life."[12]

The Bishop of Urgell is one of the princes of Andorra and one of only two Catholic bishops who still exercise temporal sovereignty, the other being the pope. The second Prince of Andorra is the President of France, who inherited the title from the kings of France. Thanks to a set of historical arrangement,s the last remnant of the Frankish March is the only monarchy presided over by joint monarchs.

After the death of Charlemagne in 814, the border counts assumed greater power and eventually broke their ties with the kings of the Franks altogether. The Umayyad emirs of Cordoba, who by this time had conquered all of Andalusia, did not pose a serious threat. Even after victory in the civil war they could exert but little authority over the provincial governors and some could not make their will felt beyond Cordoba. Andalusia became in effect a federation of autonomous states whose rulers were certainly not a threat to Europe anymore. Indeed, they were hardly a threat to the Christian principalities of the north, which were firmly entrenched thanks to internal tensions, the intervention of the Franks and the protection afforded by the hostile mountains of Cantabria and the Pyrenees. That is not to say Muslim forces were no longer a match for the princes of the North. Emir Abdul Rahman II rallied enough support to arrest the southward advance of King Alphonse II of Asturias in 798, give aid to Aquitanians rebelling against Charles, and sack Barcelona in 851. Still, the Moors were no longer capable of threatening the Franks as they had done at Toulouse, Tours, and in Septimania.

As mentioned, the counts of the marches tended to act independently of the West Frankish kings who generally showed little interest in the Iberian frontier and in time they claimed formal independence. The kingdoms of Aragon and Navarre emerged from the marches, and the County of Barcelona increased in strength and became the Principality of Catalonia. Asturias remained strong and changed its name from the Kingdom of Leon when the capital moved from Oviedo to Leon in 910. These new and independent states became bases of the *Reconquista*, the restoration of Christian rule to all of Hispania. Asturias would later become the Kingdom of Castile, which joined in a dynastic union with Aragon in the 15th century and became the foundation of Spain as we know it today. The Catalonian counties and Navarre would be absorbed into Aragon and a new Christian kingdom, Portugal, would emerge in the eleventh and twelfth centuries.

Meanwhile, the dominant Umayyad emirs saw themselves not only as the lawful rulers of Andalusia but as heirs to the caliphate, and in 929 a successor of Abdul Raman I, Abdul Raman III, took the final step in severing the tenuous ties with the caliphate by proclaiming himself Successor to the Prophet and Commander of the Faithful: "We are the most worthy to fulfill our right, and the most entitled to complete our good fortune, and to put on the clothing granted by the nobility of God, because of the favour which He has shown us, and the renown which He has given us, and the power to which He has raised us, because of what He has enabled us to acquire, and because of what He has made easy for us and for our state to achieve; He has made our name and the greatness of our power celebrated everywhere; and He has made the hopes of the worlds

---

[12] Augustin, Byron (September 1, 2008). *Andorra*. Marshall Cavendish. p. 24.

depend on us, and made their errings turn again to us and their rejoicing at good news be about our dynasty. And praise be to God, possessed of grace and kindness, for the grace which He has shown, [God] most worthy of superiority for the superiority which He has granted us. We have decided that the da'wa should be to us as Commander of the Faithful and that letters emanating from us or coming to us should be [headed] in the same manner."[13]

The period of the Cordoban Caliphate is commonly regarded as an Andalusian golden age. During this time, Cordoba, boasting 500 000 inhabitants, overtook Constantinople as the most populous city in Europe.[14] This was due in no small part to advances in irrigation and animal husbandry, and trade in luxury items such as gold, silk and ceramics increased Andalusia's prosperity. Andalusia exported much grain, oil and other foodstuffs, and it traded in all the major ports of the Mediterranean, both Muslim and Christian. Cordoba also became a great cultural center and the celebrated polymath Ibn Rushd (Averroes) called the city home. His commentaries of Aristotle were translated into Latin by western Christian philosophers and theologians, notably Thomas of Aquinas, whose writings provided a framework for Christian theology to the present day. Andalusia was also home to Al-Zahrawi (Abulcasis), the "father of modern surgery."[15] Like Ibn Rushd, he was considered the greatest authority on his subject by Muslims and Christians alike, and his works were widely translated into Latin.

During the caliphate the number of Muslims in Andalusia increased, not principally through conversion but by migration from North Africa and the parts of Iberia in the north conquered by the Christian successor states of Asturias and the Frankish March. Nevertheless, they remained in the minority, except in Cordoba and other urban centers. Christians were left in peace by and large, though they tended to be dealt more harshly than Muslims by the judiciary. Jews numbered around 10% of the population, comparable to the number of Berber Muslims.

The glory of the Umayyads did not last forever, as they were beset by factions. The Caliph became a mere figurehead while real power lay with the emirs of the provinces and the *hajib* (first minister). In 1009, civil war erupted between adherents of rival caliphs and lasted until 1031 and the Christian states to the north unsurprisingly supported the rival factions in order to hasten the decline of the Andalusian state. The last Umayyad Caliph Hisham III was deposed in 1031 after he tried to raise taxes on a population burdened by more than two decades of war. There was no one left with the strength and support to unite Andalusia, and it dissolved into a number of *taifas* or factions, each ruled by an emir. The largest of them were centered at Toledo, Saragossa, and Badajoz, with most hugging the southern and eastern seaboards.

---

[13] Wasserstein, David (1993). *The Caliphate in the West: An Islamic Political Institution in the Iberian Peninsula* (snippet view). Oxford: Clarendon Press. p. 11.

[14] Chandler, Tertius. *Four Thousand Years of Urban Growth: An Historical Census* (1987), St. David's University Press.

[15] Ahmad, Z. (St Thomas' Hospital) (2007), "Al-Zahrawi - The Father of Surgery", *ANZ Journal of Surgery*, 77 (Suppl. 1): A83

The Christian states naturally took advantage of their disunity, and King Ferdinand I of Leon was able to unite the Christians against the Moors. By the time of his death in 1065, Ferdinand, calling himself Emperor of All Hispania, had reduced Toledo, Saragossa, Badajoz, and Seville to the status of vassals, and had extended his borders almost to the banks of the Tagus River. Ferdinand's son, Alphonso VI, built upon these victories, and in 1085 conquered Toledo and absorbed the largest taifa into his domain.

The fall of Toledo convinced the emirs that they were all in danger of losing their territories. They then requested Yusuf ibn Tashfin, the Almoravid Emir of the Maghreb, to come to their aid. The call was probably motivated by desperation, given the severe reputation of the Almoravids. The luxurious lifestyle of the taifa emirs and their tolerant, even servile, attitude toward their Christian neighbors were hardly likely to endear them to the fundamentalist Almoravids. Perhaps the emirs half-hoped Yusuf would not respond, or if he came, would leave shortly after defeating the Christian princes. But he did respond, crossing the Straits of Gibraltar with an army in 1086. A joint force defeated the kings of Leon, Castile, and Aragon at the Battle of Sagrajas, northeast of Badajoz, on October 23, 1086. More than half the Christian army was lost to Yusuf's fanatical swordsmen and javelin throwers, but the Moorish casualties were also heavy, and they could not follow up on their victory. The remainder of the Christians retired but without suffering any sizeable loss of territory. Even their grand prize, Toledo, remained in Castilian hands. Nevertheless, the Moors had achieved their aim: the Christian advance had been checked.

It must have been with some relief that the emirs saw Yusuf return to his homeland, but if they hoped he would stay there, their hopes were dashed. The indolence and corruption of the emirs offended them, and it took little for Yusuf to convince his followers to return and subjugate them. But there was an obstacle. Islamic law forbade war against fellow Muslims, and Yusuf was nothing if not devout. But the clerical scholars obligingly issued a *fatwa* (judgment) declaring that the corrupt taifa emirs were heretics and therefore not true Muslims. Between 1090 and 1094 Almoravid armies conquered all the taifas except for Saragossa, and Andalusia was absorbed into the Almoravid Empire and ruled from Marrakesh.

The End of Muslim Rule in Andalusia

Toward the middle of the 12th century the Maghreb was in turmoil. The Almoravids were in retreat before a regime even more fanatically religious and this was the Almohads, "those who profess the unity of God." They were restrictive in their faith that they believed the Almoravids were heretics and by 1146 the Almohads had conquered the western Maghreb (Morocco) and were invading Andalusia. They gradually conquered it from the Almoravids over more than two decades. Observing the war between the Muslim factions, Pope Eugene III proclaimed a crusade against the Moors in 1147 and for a time the crusaders enjoyed important gains. Lisbon fell in 1147, followed by the rich ports of Almeria and Tortosa, the last succumbing in 1149.

The regime of the Almohad caliphs was more enduring than its predecessors, and they were the last rulers to unite all of Muslim Iberia. At first, they drove Christians and Jews north as the Almoravids had done, but in time they moderated their fanaticism. The Muslims in Andalusia were always a small proportion of the population, and it was bad economic management to persecute important members of the community such as merchants, financiers and landowners.

Despite the first successes of the Christian states and crusaders, the Almohads for a time not only held the Christian kings at bay but seriously damaged them. Caliph Abu Yusuf left Marrakesh to meet an invasion of King Alphonso VIII of Castile and he soundly defeated the Christian prince at Alarcos on July 18, 1195. However, 17 years later this victory was reversed at Las Navas de Tolosa on July 16, 1212. Alphonso VIII led an alliance of the Christian princes against the Almohads and the majority of the 30 000 Muslim warriors perished while the Christians suffered the loss of 2000. The Moors never recovered from the disaster, and the Christian states were emboldened to advance south, with the support of the Catholic Church, which encouraged them to liberate the Christians living under Moorish tyranny. The weakening of central power led to the revival of the taifas and by 1238 the Almohad domain in Andalusia was reduced to the coastal region around Granada. By this time their rule in Morocco was confined to the capital Marrakesh, and so when Muhammad of the Nasrid dynasty expelled the last Almohad governor and proclaimed himself Emir of Granada, there was no revenge to be feared.

All the while, the *Reconquista* continued, and there was no Muslim state powerful enough to resist the Kingdom of Castile. The emirs of Granada saved themselves by paying tribute to the Christian state from 1246, mostly in the form of gold that came from Africa and they also provided troops for Castile's military campaigns. But it was an uncomfortable relationship. The Muslim nobles baulked at being obliged to submit to Christians and the Castilians distrusted them. War broke out between the two states several times, and in 1340 Emir Yusuf called upon Abu Al-Hasan, the Marinid Sultan of Morocco, to help him to overthrow the Castilians and end the ignominy of the last Andalusian state. The Moroccan prince amassed a huge army of 60 000 men and took Gibraltar from Castile in preparation for an invasion. He intended to break the power of the Christian kingdom and restore a Muslim power base in Iberia.

The threat was serious. The Castilian fleet was destroyed and the Marinid army crossed the Straits unencumbered. Alphonso XI of Castile and Alphonso IV of Portugal could only raise 20 000 troops between them and they engaged Abu Al-Hasan and Yusuf at Rio Salado on the southern coast of Iberia on October 30, 1340.

The Marinid invasion was the last attempt by Muslims to dominate the Iberian Peninsula but from 1340 its future was dictated by Christianity and by Castile. Granada survived for another 152 years, protected by the Sierra Nevada ranges and by its importance as a trading center with Africa, but when the Portuguese began to establish oceanic trading routes with Africa, Granada lost its value as a trading partner.

The centuries of smaller conflicts between the caliphate and the Christian kingdoms culminated with the Granada War, which would last from 1482-1491. There were multiple incidents that resulted in bringing about the war, but the situation escalated drastically when Granada violated the truce of 1478 by attacking Zahara in December 1481 as punishment for a Christian raid that occurred a few months prior. Zahara was overtaken, and the population became slaves in the kingdom.

In response to that, support for war grew in Andalusia, and several factions plotted a counterstrike that would lead to a greater war. The Granada War officially began after the city of Alhama was seized and war was endorsed by the ruling caliphate. The caliphate tried to retake Alhambra but was thwarted by Castile and Aragon in April 1482.[16]

Castile and Aragon had been permanently fused about 15 years earlier by the marriage between Queen Isabella of Castile and Ferdinand of Aragon. Both kingdoms were facing internal rebellions as Isabella and Ferdinand came of age. When Ferdinand was a small child, the conflict between his father, Juan, and his older brother, Carlos, led to civil war between Aragon and the mountainous region of Catalonia. He joined his father on the battlefield during his early adolescence and continued to fight alongside him for several years, thereby honing his skills in battle and as a wartime commander in his own right. In 1468, Juan crowned Ferdinand King of Sicily, hoping to improve his marriage prospects, particularly in light of a hoped-for match with Isabella of Castile.

King Juan of Aragon first proposed a marital alliance between his son Ferdinand and Isabella of Castile in 1467, prior to the Treaty of Toros de Guisando. The proposed marriage was of great strategic advantage for Aragon, as it could provide a potential end to the conflict between Castile and Aragon. His attempt to negotiate a marriage at that time was unsuccessful, but he continued to press his cause, including making Ferdinand King of Sicily to improve his status. When he repeated his offer in 1468, it privately came with the promise of Aragon's money and troops. Juan's ambassador, Peralta, visited Isabella, sneaking into her rooms at night and sharing the king's offer with her.

---

[16] William H. Prescott, *The Art of War in Spain: The Conquest of Granada, 1481–1492*, edited by Albert D. McJoynt, (London: Greenhill Books, 1995).

Ferdinand and Isabella

In early 1469, Isabella made her decision and planned to move forward with a marriage to Ferdinand of Aragon. While Isabella acted independently when she agreed to the marriage contract with Ferdinand, in many ways the betrothal was much like other royal engagements; the two young royals had never met and were planning to marry solely for political reasons. But for Isabella this was a better match than the previous suggestions, since Ferdinand was her own age, attractive, and well-regarded. Both spoke Spanish, making communication feasible, and they shared many native customs and cultural practices. On top of all that, they were closely related; as second cousins, they would, like many other royals, require a papal dispensation to marry.

The royal marriage agreement, negotiated by Carrillo and Ambassador Peralta, included a number of restrictions on Ferdinand and his role in the Castilian government. While he was expected to serve as her military commander, he could not make civil or ecclesiastical appointments and had to have Isabella's permission to leave the country. Isabella was guaranteed generous gifts upon her marriage, but most would not be delivered until her older brother Enrique died or was removed from the throne and she became queen.

There was an overriding issue that seemed to be a potential elephant in the room: how would the two rule jointly? While the two had rarely quarreled, Isabella clearly expected that Ferdinand's ego would be bruised and that he would respond to his own less significant role in Castile with anger. Raised in Aragon, he may not have even supported the idea of female succession. Isabella planned a celebration for his arrival at the court in Castile and ordered him treated with the greatest respect to smooth over any hurt feelings, but it was not enough. Despite the fact their marriage agreement had specified Ferdinand's role in Castile, the two continued to argue over the division of power within the kingdom for several months.

Isabella finally agreed to call a council to discuss and provide a decision on the matter of female succession, but she convinced Ferdinand to support her as queen before the council met by pointing out that their interests were the same, and that if a female could not succeed to the throne, it would disqualify their only child, Isabel. With that, the two soon began to function as co-regents, adopting their own coat of arms and the motto "Tanto Monta" ("One is equal to the other"), marking both their role as regents and the respect within their marriage, negotiated in the months following their coronation.

The Coat of Arms

One of the reasons they quickly put aside their differences was that they faced plenty of external enemies. In fact, Ferdinand and Isabella continued to struggle for their mutual right to the throne of Castile even after Enrique's death because Enrique's allies, including the King of Portugal, continued to favor Princess Juana over Isabella. The longstanding tensions between Ferdinand and Carrillo also came to a head, and he left their cout to join the King of Portugal and Princess Juana in battle against them. Ferdinand and Isabella continued to be financially strained, but they still prepared for war with Portugal, relying upon their own supporters to fund an army. Both worked ceaselessly, but they were deeply grieved when Isabella miscarried a male child in May 1475.

During the summer of 1475, Ferdinand and Isabella suffered a significant military defeat against the Portuguese army at Toro. However, the situation improved that autumn when the Church, with the support of the prelates, lent the couple a substantial amount of wealth, finally ending their financial struggles. King Juan of Aragon also sent artillery, building equipment and his son, Alonso of Aragon, an experienced general, to assist them. Ferdinand, a fine soldier himself, now had the resources he needed to be victorious against Portugal.

The following January, Isabella signed peace treaties with Afonso of Portugal, but it was short lived, as Afonso of Portugal continued his attempts to gain control of Spain by seeking an alliance with the French king, Louis XI. Small Portuguese forces remained in Castile even after the treaty was signed, forcing Ferdinand and Isabella to grant clemency to rebelling nobles, including Carrillo himself, in an attempt to gain the loyalty of the entire Spanish nobility and support for their reign.

With the rebels no longer as big of an issue, Isabella and Ferdinand succeeded in negotiating favorable terms for peace between Castile and France, thereby eliminating any possible alliance between France and Portugal against them. However, the terms for peace between France and Aragon remained significantly less favorable than those between France and Castile. They also maintained the support of the pope, who retracted the dispensation allowing the betrothal of Afonso of Portugal and Princess Juana, striking another blow against their enemies.

As the war finally came to an end, Juan of Aragon died in early 1479, and Isabella and Ferdinand thus became monarchs of a much larger kingdom. In June of 1479, Ferdinand returned to Aragon to manage their affairs, while another round of peace negotiations with Portugal, led by Isabella, forced Princess Juana to join a convent, permanently eliminating any threat to her reign.

Following the war, Isabella set to improving conditions in Spain. She eliminated all but five mints in the country, standardizing coinage and preserving the value of Spanish money, which helped to correct some of the economic challenges in Castile. She also reorganized the judicial and administrative systems, and her new judicial system, the Hermandades, reduced crime throughout Castile and brought peace and order to the kingdom. In 1477, she even sat as magistrate herself, aided by legal clerks, in Seville. Ferdinand was often away, managing Castilian troops against the Portuguese or leading the defenses of Aragon against the French while Isabella managed the internal affairs of the state independently. Isabella created the consejo real or high council, to help govern the country, and these council members were expected to remain with the court at all times, traveling with Isabella as she moved throughout the kingdom. While the final decision on matters of state rested with Isabella, the council provided support, advice and could govern if she was unavailable. Furthermore, a separate council with somewhat more power was created to rule non-Castilian lands, including Aragon and Sicily, which enabled Ferdinand to live primarily in Castile.

Once these critical social issues had been managed, Isabella looked to the state treasury. Depleted by Enrique's generous bequests to the nobility, the Castilian government was lacking essential sources of revenue. Between 1480 and 1482, Isabella and Ferdinand reclaimed a number of properties granted to the Spanish nobility by Enrique, which both improved financial well-being of the state (by returning income to the treasury) and limited the power of the nobility. To maintain loyalty, Isabella allowed the Spanish nobles to retain some insignificant and largely symbolic powers and privileges, including the right to wear hats in the presence of the king and queen.

While Isabella negotiated treaties and managed affairs of state, she was often pregnant. In the summer of 1478, Isabella delivered a boy, named Juan after his grandfathers. He would inherit both Aragon and Castile, providing the much-needed male heir for their kingdom. Isabella kept Juan with her, as the boy was somewhat sickly, causing her to worry significantly. The following year, in November, Isabella delivered her third child, a girl.

During these years, the measures imposed by Isabella vastly improved the conditions in Castile for many of the people, allowing them access to basic goods, and the improved finances of the state also allowed for better roads and other forms of infrastructure. The courts dispensed harsh punishments, but the rule of law prevailed and violence was reduced throughout Castile. The nobles were somewhat less pleased by the changes, having lost both property and income, but Isabella had proven herself to be a competent administrator. Ferdinand, as the head of the army, had helped to achieve peace with their neighbors.

The two of them were a good match for the throne and good rulers for most of their people, but it was about to become painstakingly clear that the kindness and generosity only extended to Christians.

In 1478, King Ferdinand and Queen Isabella created The Tribunal of the Holy Office of the Inquisition – in short, the Spanish Inquisition. The monarchs viewed the inquisition as crucial for a number of reasons. Isabella had only resumed the throne to Castile 2 years prior, and she found herself engaged in conflict with the Queen of Portugal, Juana la Beltraneja. The French and Portuguese support of Beltraneja meant a trio of forces were actively working to overthrow her. Isabella hoped to combat this by centralizing their power through religious unity. Furthermore, the inquisition hoped to diminish other rival political powers, including that of the

Jews.

While the Inquisition was being implemented, King Ferdinand and Queen Isabella set their eyes on the city of Loja, but they failed to take it. At the same time, Abu Hasan's son renamed himself Emir Muhammad XII and rebelled, plunging the caliphate into chaos. The civil war would last until roughly 1483, when Emir Muhammad XII would be captured by Christians at Lucena.

Emir Muhammad XII

Ferdinand and Isabella, who had not been planning on taking the entirety of Granada, decided to make Emir Muhammad XII an ally. They agreed to release Emir Muhammad XII on the condition that he wage war against his father and become a pseudo-Christian ally that would give the Christian kingdoms the extra push they needed to drive out the caliphate.

The agreement between the Catholic monarchs and Emir Muhammad XII lasted until roughly 1485, when Emir Muhammad XII was defeated by his own uncle, al-Zagal. Al-Zagal became the new leader of the caliphate after kicking out his older brother, who died shortly afterwards from old age. With that, Emir Muhammad XII fled back to the Christian kingdoms.

Meanwhile, dissent, and distrust continued to build and foment among the Muslim forces, which made them ineffective at protecting Granada. The town would be seized by one of Ferdinand's greatest allies, the Marquis of Cádiz, and shortly afterwards, the Marquis would claim the cities of Ronda and Marbella through a combination of military might and negotiations with the city leaders. In Marbella, the Christians managed to get their hands on part of the impressive Granadan fleet.[17]

Emir Muhammad XII would enter the scene again, this time spending the next three years convincing the Muslim population to support peace with the Christian kingdoms and their rule by claiming the Christians would be lenient, provide better opportunities, and be willing to allow the Muslim citizenry to continue practicing their religion. Christian support subsequently grew among peoples of all religious backgrounds.

The next major event in the final act of the *Reconquista* was the siege of Málaga by the Castilians in 1487. The caliphate was slow to respond to the attack, and when they did, they were unable to drive away the Christian armies. This was because the general, Emir al-Zagal, was forced to leave the majority of his forces behind to fight the civil war, and there were not enough troops to counter the stronger Castilian army.

The first part of the city to capitulate was also the first to be attacked: Vélez-Málaga. Castilian forces were aided by local Muslim supporters of Emir Muhammad XII, who had returned to his original name of Baobdil by this point in time. The city switched hands on April 27, 1487.

The rest of Málaga continued to fight as sections of the city slowly fell, surrendered, or switched sides in the conflict. The commander of the region decided it was better to die in battle than capitulate to the enemy and thus continued to fight viciously against the Christians. The African garrison in the region and Christians who had converted to Islam were among those on the front lines, and they attacked with almost suicidal ferociousness out of fear of what Ferdinand and his commanders would do when Málaga fell.

From May-August 1487, they threw everything they had into the war effort before eventually conceding defeat. As they may have suspected, when the Muslim leaders of Málaga tried to surrender, Ferdinand refused because his offer had previously been rejected twice. Once Málaga fell, Ferdinand marched in and enslaved the majority of the population, including Christians who had remained behind. Many of the renegades and Christians who had converted to Islam faced death by being burned alive or stabbed repeatedly with reeds. The only people spared were the Jews, who had been ransomed by Castilian Jews in good faith.[18]

---

[17] Ibid.
[18] Ibid.

The fall of Málaga was arguably the most significant event during the Granada War. Málaga was the most crucial port held by the caliphate for the Granadan fleet, and without it, their ships would be unable to keep a foothold in the region. Without the fleet, Muslim forces lost their most significant assets, leaving them unable to attack the Christian kingdoms by sea or bring extra supplies to Granada.

After the loss of Málaga, al-Zagal's reputation was destroyed, and Muhammad XII was able to claim Granada as people transferred to his cause. Al-Zagal then lost Vélez-Rubio, Vélez-Blanco, and Vera, but he still controlled some of the major cities. Meanwhile, Muhammad XII gladly handed over some of the territory to the Christians in the belief it would be given back once the war was over. He would be dead wrong.

Starting in 1489, the Christians started to lay siege to Baza, which was the last remaining stronghold of al-Zagal in the region. The city was one of the most defensible in Granada and forced the Christians to divide their army into several different groups to try to wrap around the city and hit its weakest points. Artillery didn't help because of the thickness of the walls and the roughness of the terrain, which made it difficult to push or carry heavy weaponry. The Christians did not have enough money to supply and pay the Castilian soldiers, and many troops had to be threatened with torture and death to keep them from deserting. Queen Isabella, in an effort to improve morale, visited the site of the siege herself.

Ultimately, al-Zagal surrendered after six months of prolonged attacks. Even though his garrison was mostly untouched, he saw no reason to continue to resist. He was able to negotiate a peaceful and generous surrender, and the city's population was left in peace.

The Muslim forces were now almost completely out of Granada, but it would take one last major push to get them out of the Iberian Peninsula.

Al-Zagal ended up in Christian captivity, leaving the Muslims in Granada without a competent military strategist. Without him, it seemed like the final conquest of Granada would be quick, easy, and painless for the Christians. However, by assuming there would be no more resistance, Ferdinand and Isabella failed to compensate their allies appropriately.[19] Muhammad XII was furious that the land that was supposed to go to him continued to be controlled by the administration of Castile, and in response, he violently ended his vassalage and led his forces against the Christian kingdoms.

Unfortunately for Muhammad XII, he held territory that would prove difficult to control. He still held Granada and the Alpujarra Mountains, which featured harsh terrain and an almost indefensible city because of its geography and the positions of Christian troops around it.[20]

---

[19] L.P. Harvey, *Muslims in Spain, 1500 to 1614*, (Chicago: University of Chicago Press, 2005), pg. 385.
[20] Prescott, *The Art of War in Spain*.

Despite low odds of success, Muhammad XII persisted and sent messengers with letters to Egypt begging for assistance. The Egyptians, although sympathetic to the plight of the Muslims in Iberia, could not help - by the end of the 15th century, Egypt faced near constant warfare with the nearby Ottoman Turks, who were rapidly forming their own empire in the Middle East. To further complicate matters, Castile and Aragon were valuable allies against the Ottomans, making it untenable for Egypt to break their alliance to assist Muhammad XII. The Sultan of Egypt wrote to Ferdinand expressing his disappointment with the Christian kingdoms, but that was all.

After that, Muhammad XII tried to convince the Kingdom of Fez to help him, but it's unclear how the administrators responded. Even North Africa failed to assist the remaining Muslims in Iberia as they continued to supply the Christian kingdoms with wheat and other trade goods.[21] To make the situation worse, the Muslims no longer controlled any coastline and could not receive aid from North Africa. The *Reconquista* was almost complete.

Ferdinand and Isabella launched the final siege of Granada in April 1491. The siege would last for eight months, and the situation within the city would only worsen as internal enemies aided the Christians and Muhammad XII's advisors feuded with one another for control. Historians would later determine that at least one advisor was a Castilian spy and several others were receiving numerous bribes to help the city fall. Eventually, Muhammad XII admitted defeat and signed a surrender document, the Treaty of Granada, which was heavily provisional. The treaty officially went into effect on November 25, 1491, and granted Granada two months to get its affairs in order.

It took the entire two months for the administration to kick out the traitors and develop some semblance of normalcy. Riots were common, and many people were caught attempting to flee the territory. Several crucial administrators were found assassinated.

On January 2, 1492, the treaty officially went into effect. Castilian forces flooded the city of Granada and confiscated Alhambra, securing the last Muslim-owned state in the Al-Andalus. By noon that morning, the Christian soldiers had evicted most of its previous residents. Moorish flags were removed and replaced with Christian and Castilian flags, and banners strung up in the tallest towers. Most symbolic of all was the giant silver cross that was placed on the highest roof of the Comares Tower, sending out an unmistakable message: the Castilians, along with Catholicism, were here to stay.

On July 30 of that same year, as mentioned in the diary of Christopher Columbus, the Castilians published an edict that expelled close to 200,000 Jews from Spain. Tens of thousands of these refugees died en route to their new destinations. This pivotal expulsion was one of the

---

[21] J.N. Hillgarth, *The Spanish Kingdoms: 1250–1516. Volume II: 1410–1516, Castilian Hegemony*, (Oxford: Oxford University Press, 1978), pg. 386.

"pet projects" backed by the Spanish Inquisition. In this petrifying climate, the Muslims of Granada dared not leave their homes. Later that day, Muhammad II was driven out of Alhambra. It was said that upon his exit, he cocked his head back to steal a final glimpse of the palace and fortress, only to be reprimanded by his scowling mother, who snapped, "Do not cry like a woman for that which you could not defend as a man."

Upon the outset of this unfamiliar reign, the Muslims were relieved to hear that freedom of worship would be tolerated, and certain leniency would be granted to them to ease them into the new rule. Only, the Castilians would soon fall short on their word. Following a foiled rebellion in the late 1490s, Queen Isabella announced that she would be revoking all laws of tolerance against the Muslims. From 1502 onward, Muslims who wished to avoid execution were presented with 2 choices – convert to Christianity, or leave. Hundreds of thousands fled from Granada, mostly to Africa, while others embraced their new Christian faiths as "Moriscos," as the Spanish called them. A small fraction stayed behind, taking their worship underground.

Authorities placed the remaining Muslims under strict surveillance, and at the same time, were on the constant lookout for secret Muslims. On Thursday nights and Friday mornings, Moriscos were made to leave their doors open, so that passing soldiers could inspect their houses. Any Morisco who was seen bathing or thought to be suspiciously clean would be apprehended, as Muslim tradition required baths before prayer congregations on Fridays. Those caught red-handed with a Quran were slain on the spot. Stories also surfaced about Castilians kidnapping Muslim children to raise them as Christians behind closed doors.

The Muslims suffered increasingly suffocating restrictions. They were buried under hefty taxes and prohibited from wearing Muslim garb. They were to speak in only Spanish, and those that could not were to find a way to grasp the language within a 3 year period. Many saw their properties seized by Castilian authorities. All Muslim documents were declared null and void.

In the weeks following the conquest of Granada, many of the structures in Granada had their coats of bright Arabesque paints and designs scrubbed and filed off. The freshly sanded facades were then awoken with whitewash, a cost-effective mixture of lime and water used to paint walls a pristine white. The Moorish-style furniture was dismantled and replaced with house fittings and fixtures that better suited the conflicting tastes of the new rulers.

The Christians launched a campaign to remove all traces of the Muslim presence to the best of their ability. Mosques and bathhouses were torn down and rebuilt as churches, convents, and monasteries. In place of the grand mosque stood a stately new cathedral. This same cathedral has since been replaced with the Church of Santa Maria de la Alhambra.

Even so, what was left of the quickly diminishing Muslims managed to stay in the shadows, and they survived under this brutal authority for over a century, until the new Christian authorities put another foot down by ordering all Muslims out of their land. For three days in

1609, all the Moriscos were forced to pack their belongings and board ships destined for the Ottoman Empire or other North African destinations. The Edict of Expulsion was signed on April 9, 1609, and it read:

> "First, that all the Andalusīs in the Kingdom of Valencia, men and women, with their children and within three days from the proclamation of this decree, remove themselves from the lands in which they currently inhabit and embark on a ship from the coast, at a place that is specifically designated for this purpose. They may only take with them from their possessions and moveable property that which they can carry. They are to embark on the ships and the galleys that have been assigned to transport them to North Africa. They are to transport them without any harm being inflicted on their person or possessions and they are to provide them with adequate food for the journey. As for they who seek to carry what they can, let them do so. Whoever deviates from this command, let them be put to death.

> "As for whoever remains [from the Moriscos], tarrying in the land, after three days from the proclamation of this order it is permissible for any who encounter them to plunder their goods and to turn them over to the authorities; if they resist, it is permissible to put them to death.[22]

> "The king commanded that the lives and the property of the Moors be protected.

> "Let it be known that the King's only intent is to remove them from our kingdom to North Africa. Let them not be harmed by word or deed or in any way. When they have arrived, let ten of them return to inform the others [that they had safely arrived in North Africa]. Let this be proclaimed to all the commanders and captains of the ships and galleys so they may implement this order.

> "Yet those who refused to obey the king's edict were removed from the royal protection."

All Moorish descendants were affected, save certain families who were permitted to stay to prevent the extinction of towns in Moorish-majority areas and children under 16. Even then, the children would be baptized if they had been so already and obliged to live under strict Catholic supervision. To spare the public purse, the Moors taken to ports were obliged to pay for their own expulsion and were then taken to the Maghreb coast and abandoned. The Spanish government had made no arrangements with the local rulers, and the Moriscos were often mistaken for invaders and attacked.

Horrified at the fate of the first deportees, the Morisco, where the densest population lived,

---

[22] https://ballandalus.wordpress.com/2015/06/29/the-royal-edict-of-expulsion-1609-and-the-last-andalusi-muslims-moriscos-of-spain/

rebelled against the expulsion. This rebellion would be the last armed conflict between the indigenous Moors and the Spanish. 21,000 Moriscos took up arms in the valleys of Valencia, but by the end of November 1609 the rebellion had been crushed.

By 1614, all the Moors in Spain had been expelled, and the deportees in North Africa were treated like strangers in a foreign land. They did not speak the language, and though they had been accused of being secret Muslims, they could not have seemed like it to the natives. After all, they had lived with Christianity forced upon them for three or four generations, and many were in fact sincere Christians who had been expelled simply because they were Moors.

A number of Moriscos became pirates and plundered the coasts of their former homeland and others joined the armies of Morocco and the Ottoman Empire. Some journeyed to friendlier parts of Europe.

For centuries after the expulsion, Moorish poets like Mahmoud Darwish pined for their renowned homeland:

"How do I write above the clouds my kin's will? And my kin
leave time behind as they leave their coats in the houses, and my kin
whenever they build a fortress they raze it to erect above it
a tent of longing for the early palm trees. My kin betray my kin
in wars of defending salt. But Granada is gold
and silken words embroidered with almonds, silver tears in
the oud string. Granada is for the great ascension to herself…
and she can be however she desires to be: the longing for
anything that has passed or will pass: a swallow's wing scratches
a woman's breast in bed, and she screams: Granada is my body.
A man loses his gazelle in the wilderness and screams: Granada is my country.
And I come from there. So sing for the sparrows to build from my ribs
a stairway to the proximal sky. Sing the gallantry of those ascending to their fate
moon by moon in the lovers' alley. Sing the birds of the garden
stone by stone. How I love you, you, who tore me
string by string on her way to her hot night … sing!
There is no morning for coffee's scent after you, sing my departure
from the cooing of pigeons on your knees, and from my soul's nest
in the letters of your easy name, Granada is for song, so sing!"[23]

A few Moriscos even returned to Spain, and not all the Moriscos had been expelled because the expulsion had been conducted in a somewhat inefficient manner. The expulsion of baptized children also presented a problem, for according to Spanish and Catholic law, they could not be

---

[23] https://molossus.wordpress.com/2009/12/14/mahmoud-darwish/

delivered into the hands of unbelievers. A great many children may have been deported to Catholic France instead, and it would be fair to assume that some kind Spaniards protected or hid the children of Moriscos.

In general, the expulsion was supported by the Spanish population, though some, like Miguel de Cervantes, author of *Don Quixote*, were not unsympathetic to the plight of the Moriscos. Cervantes put these words in the mouth of Ricote, a Moor in *Don Quixote* who has secretly returned to Spain: "You know very well, O Sancho Panza, my neighbor and friend, how the proclamation and edict that His Majesty issues against those of my race brought terror and fear to all of us…It seems to me it was divine inspiration that moved His Majesty to put into effect so noble a resolution, not because all of us were guilty, for some were firm and true Christians, though these were so few they could not oppose those who were not, but because it is not a good idea to nurture a snake in your bosom or shelter enemies in your house. In short, it was just and reasonable for us to be chastised with the punishment of exile: lenient and mild, according to some, but for us it was the most terrible we could have received. No matter where we are we weep for Spain, for, after all, we were born here and it is our native country."

Persecution of the Moriscos in Spain continued into the 18th century, and the last major punitive campaign, which inflicted only light sentences, occurred in 1727. In 1799, a treaty with Morocco guaranteed the rights of Moorish former slaves to observe the tenets of their religion in exchange for the same granted to Spanish Catholics living in Morocco. In the 19th century Spain abolished slavery, and in 1834 the Spanish Inquisition was definitively abolished, though by that stage it had virtually no authority left. The Edict of Expulsion of 1609 has never been rescinded, nor the descendants of Moriscos invited to return, though the Alhambra Decree, expelling the Jews in 1492, was formally annulled on December 16, 1968.

It is strange that a nation so profoundly influenced by its Muslim history and culture should have been so vehement in attempting to expunge it, but either way, Spain could not fully eradicate the Moors' influence. The Moors' legacy can be found in Spain's language, architecture, art, music, cuisine and customs. Ironically, the presence of Arabic scientific discoveries, particularly related to astronomy, shipbuilding, and mapmaking, allowed the Christian kingdoms of Spain and Portugal to gain an advantage over other European powers like the Netherlands, France, and Great Britain, which would take longer to cross the Atlantic Ocean and reach the New World. The intense fervor for Christianity present in the Iberian kingdoms would also have lasting implications in the Americas, where Spanish missionaries in particular were ordered to convert indigenous peoples by any means necessary, including the kinds of torture, persecution, and death reminiscent of the methods used against the Muslims and Jews at the end of the *Reconquista*. Even in the 21st century, Catholicism continues to be the most common religion throughout South America and Latin America.

Online Resources

<u>Other books about Islamic history</u> by Charles River Editors

<u>Other titles about the Moors</u> on Amazon

Further Reading

Bosworth, C.E. (1993). "Muʿāwiya II". In Bosworth, C. E.; van Donzel, E.; Heinrichs, W. P. & Pellat, Ch. (eds.). The Encyclopaedia of Islam, New Edition, Volume VII: Mif–Naz. Leiden: E. J. Brill. pp. 268–269. ISBN 90-04-09419-9.

Christides, Vassilios (2000). "ʿUkba b. Nāfiʿ". In Bearman, P. J.; Bianquis, Th.; Bosworth, C. E.; van Donzel, E. & Heinrichs, W. P. (eds.). The Encyclopaedia of Islam, New Edition, Volume X: T–U. Leiden: E. J. Brill. pp. 789–790. ISBN 90-04-11211-1.

Crone, Patricia (1994). "Were the Qays and Yemen of the Umayyad Period Political Parties?". Der Islam. Walter de Gruyter and Co. 71 (1): 1–57. doi:10.1515/islm.1994.71.1.1. ISSN 0021-1818.

Donner, Fred M. (1981). The Early Islamic Conquests. Princeton: Princeton University Press. ISBN 9781400847877.

Duri, Abd al-Aziz (2011). Early Islamic Institutions: Administration and Taxation from the Caliphate to the Umayyads and ʿAbbāsids. Translated by Razia Ali. London and Beirut: I. B. Tauris and Centre for Arab Unity Studies. ISBN 978-1-84885-060-6.

Dixon, 'Abd al-Ameer (August 1969). The Umayyad Caliphate, 65–86/684–705: (A Political Study) (Thesis). London: University of London, SOAS.

Gibb, H. A. R. (1960). "ʿAbd Allāh ibn al-Zubayr". In Gibb, H. A. R.; Kramers, J. H.; Lévi-Provençal, E.; Schacht, J.; Lewis, B. & Pellat, Ch. (eds.). The Encyclopaedia of Islam, New Edition, Volume I: A–B. Leiden: E. J. Brill. pp. 54–55. OCLC 495469456.

Hinds, M. (1993). "Muʿāwiya I b. Abī Sufyān". In Bosworth, C. E.; van Donzel, E.; Heinrichs, W. P. & Pellat, Ch. (eds.). The Encyclopaedia of Islam, New Edition, Volume VII: Mif–Naz. Leiden: E. J. Brill. pp. 263–268. ISBN 90-04-09419-9.

Hawting, Gerald R. (2000). The First Dynasty of Islam: The Umayyad Caliphate AD 661–750 (Second ed.). London and New York: Routledge. ISBN 0-415-24072-7.

Hawting, G. R. (2000). "Umayyads". In Bearman, P. J.; Bianquis, Th.; Bosworth, C. E.; van Donzel, E. & Heinrichs, W. P. (eds.). The Encyclopaedia of Islam, New Edition, Volume X: T–U. Leiden: E. J. Brill. pp. 840–847. ISBN 90-04-11211-1.

Kaegi, Walter E. (1992). Byzantium and the Early Islamic Conquests. Cambridge: Cambridge University Press. ISBN 0-521-41172-6.

Kennedy, Hugh (2001). The Armies of the Caliphs: Military and Society in the Early Islamic State. London and New York: Routledge. ISBN 0-415-25093-5.

Kennedy, Hugh (2004). The Prophet and the Age of the Caliphates: The Islamic Near East from the 6th to the 11th Century (Second ed.). Harlow: Longman. ISBN 978-0-582-40525-7.

Kennedy, Hugh (2007). The Great Arab Conquests: How the Spread of Islam Changed the World We Live In. Philadelphia: Da Capo Press. ISBN 978-0-306-81585-0.

Della Vida, Giorgio Levi & Bosworth, Bosworth (2000). "Umayya b. Abd Shams". In Bearman, P. J.; Bianquis, Th.; Bosworth, C. E.; van Donzel, E. & Heinrichs, W. P. (eds.). The Encyclopaedia of Islam, New Edition, Volume X: T–U. Leiden: E. J. Brill. pp. 837–839. ISBN 90-04-11211-1.

Lilie, Ralph-Johannes (1976). Die byzantinische Reaktion auf die Ausbreitung der Araber. Studien zur Strukturwandlung des byzantinischen Staates im 7. und 8. Jhd (in German). Munich: Institut für Byzantinistik und Neugriechische Philologie der Universität München. OCLC 797598069.

Madelung, Wilferd (1997). The Succession to Muhammad: A Study of the Early Caliphate. Cambridge: Cambridge University Press. ISBN 0-521-56181-7.

Wellhausen, J. (1927). Weir, Margaret Graham (ed.). The Arab Kingdom and its Fall. Calcutta: University of Calcutta. ISBN 9780415209045

Free Books by Charles River Editors

We have brand new titles available for free most days of the week. To see which of our titles are currently free, click on this link.

Discounted Books by Charles River Editors

We have titles at a discount price of just 99 cents everyday. To see which of our titles are currently 99 cents, click on this link.